# Rhyming

# Dictionary

All the essential words in
an easy-to-follow format!

Alfred Music Co., Inc.
P.O. Box 10003
Van Nuys, CA 91410-0003
**alfred.com**

Copyright © MMXIII by Alfred Music Co., Inc.
All rights reserved. Printed in USA.

*No part of this book shall be reproduced, arranged, adapted, recorded, publicly
performed, stored in a retrieval system, or transmitted by any means without
written permission from the publisher. In order to comply with copyright
laws, please apply for such written permission and/or license by
contacting the publisher at alfred.com/permissions.*

ISBN-10: 0-7390-9589-7
ISBN-13: 978-0-7390-9589-8

Cover photograph by Karen Miller.

 **Alfred Cares.** Contents printed on environmentally responsible paper.

# Contents

# Introduction

Words are the tools of the modern lyricist, and this dictionary is your toolbox. Alfred's Mini Music Guide *Rhyming Dictionary* provides the most essential words and information in a portable, handy size, and it is designed with the contemporary songwriter in mind. Most words are cross-referenced in more than one place to make it quicker and easier to find the perfect word.

If you're trying to rhyme *antediluvian, odalisque,* or *ubiquitous,* you won't find it in this book. Only the most often-used words of the modern song are listed here. Every editorial or formatting decision was based on this image: it's late, you're sitting with pen in hand, and you've just written the perfect line—but you need something to rhyme with it, and you need it now. You grab this book, look up the word—and there are your rhymes. Inspired, you write the second perfect line, and on you go with your song.

This valuable toolbox of rhymes makes the development of your craft smooth and efficient. Use it to find the perfect word at just the right moment. Discover great words you've never thought of before.

# How This Book Works

Traditional rhyming books take many pages to explain how to use their book—and even then, it's still hard to find your way around. Filled with references to "masculine" versus "feminine" rhymes, "penults" versus "antepenults," and "e" sounds versus "ee" sounds, they seem only usable by English professors. Others have headings like *AK-en, IR-up, ÜR'ning* (what's that mean?), etc. Before you can find your rhyme, you've lost your inspiration—if not your mind.

# Format

Formatting this dictionary was not without its challenges. Words are cross-referenced: if you want to rhyme *bad*, look up *Bad*, and you'll find *sad*. If you want to rhyme *sad*, look up *Sad*, and find *bad*, etc. However, there are over 400 words that rhyme with *Be*. To cross-reference them as previously described would create a volume roughly the size and weight of a crosstown bus.

In these instances, a "key word" was chosen (in this example, *Be*) and all the possible words rhyming with that are listed under the key word. So, when you look up *Tea*, you find this word, and the entry looks like this:

**Tea** (see **Be**).

That means there are too many rhymes to list under all entries, and *Be* is the key word. Then, simply look up *Be*, and you'll find *Tea*, along with a few hundred common rhymes.

In the few instances where there are more than 100 rhymes for an entry, the words are grouped by syllable (one syllable, two syllable, etc.).

Remember the "key word" is often the most common, simplest word. So, if you're trying to rhyme *oscillated*, and it's not listed, look up a simpler word which rhymes with it (like *hated*). Then look at that word—there you'll find all the words you need to rhyme with *oscillated*. This situation is rare indeed, but it's helpful to keep in mind if you're trying to rhyme a large word containing many syllables.

# Broken Rules

Other rhyming dictionaries are too cumbersome for the contemporary songwriter. They have rigid rules of what rhymes, not taking into account different pronunciations or ways you can enunciate words to make them rhyme.

For example, under *Coffee* is only the word *toffee*. But in the world of pop music, *Be, Me,* etc., could work with *Coffee.* So, when you see an entry that looks like this:

**Coffee** toffee (see *be*)

it means that toffee is all that rhymes with coffee, but if you look up *Be*, indicated in italic, you'll find other words that can work in a song. This "see" cross-reference is also used when, depending on your dialect or accent, some other words are available that could possibly rhyme if pronounced in a certain way.

So, when the word following "see" is in bold:

**Among** (see **Young**)

it means that the word is offered as a "strict" rhyme; when the referenced word is in italic, it is a suggestion of other possible rhymes.

Slang words and colloquialisms are included whenever possible and appropriate. Under the word *Anchor*, for example, you'll find *thank 'er.*

# Names, Places, Expressions, and Clichés

Names (*José*), famous people (*Sigmund Freud*), and places (*Trinidad*) are often included. In general, these tend to be included for words that do *not* have many rhymes, and they tend not to be included for words that *do* have many rhymes.

Common, everyday expressions and short clichés are also included wherever possible—and, hopefully, those listed will get you thinking of others that might be found in your corner of the world but aren't included here.

# Words Left Out

In addition to words that would probably never be used in a song, a few common words were left out that had only one rhyme, if that rhyme was a word that would be extremely unusual in a pop song. For example, the only strict rhyme for *terminal* is *germinal*, which, according to *Merriam Webster's Collegiate Dictionary* means "relating to, or having the characteristic of a germ cell." This book assumes you're not, in fact, writing that great pop song about the heartache of being a germ.

Drug and sexual references are kept to a minimum. Obscene words and those words found offensive to particular ethnic groups or religions are also left out.

# The Headers

At the top of every page is a header. These headers include the first and last words of each *spread* (two facing pages). The header for the left-facing page shows the first word, and the header for the right-facing page shows the last word. This will help you find what you're looking for quicker.

In addition, the headers include a running list of the most common prefixes and suffixes. You can create more words by adding prefixes and suffixes. When you're looking at a word, look up at the header, and mix and match what's there with the word you're looking at to create other words.

The more likely it is that a word could appear in a song, the more likely it's included in the initial list. (For example, under *View*, you'll find *review* and *preview*, etc.)

If you are trying to rhyme a word that has a prefix or suffix already built in and you don't find it, don't give up! You should find it in its original form. For example, if you're looking up *viewing*, and you don't find it, simply take off the suffix (in this case, *ing*), and look up *View*. There, you'll find a list of words that only need the *"ing"* added to find the rhyme that's right for you.

# Glossary of Rhyme Schemes

Poetry is formed by a group of lines called a *stanza*, or scheme.

Many songwriters fall into a rut with regard to rhyme schemes—that is, using the same patterns over and over again. It's important to avoid this by learning and experimenting with as many rhyme schemes as possible to add variety and interest to your songs.

## The Basics

Here are a few of the most common rhyme schemes found in poetry and songs all over the world. Letters (**A**, **B**, **C**, etc.) are used to notate the scheme (the recurrence of the rhyme).

**A B C B**

**A**

Roses are red

**B**

Violets are **blue**

**C**

Sugar is sweet

**B**

And so are **you**

Here are some variations on this format.

## A B A B

**A**
Roses are **red**

**B**
Violets are **blue**

**A**
I'm quite well-**fed**

**B**
And so are **you**

## A B C A

**A**
Violets are **blue**

**B**
Roses are red

**C**
My heart is bursting

**A**
With love for **you**

**A A B A**

**A**

Violets are **blue**

**A**

As I always **knew**

**B**

But the red of the roses

**A**

Are meant only for **you**

**A A B B**

**A**

The look in your **eye**,

**A**

Violet blue, doesn't **lie**

**B**

You've been with **another**;

**B**

specifically, my **brother**

As with all rhyme schemes, there are a multitude of variations on these. While a little complicated and challenging, the following variations can be very effective.

**A B A A  B C B B**

**A**

The tick of the **clock**

**B**

Stops dead without **you**

**A**

I'm a boat without a **dock**

**A**

A shoe without a **sock**

**B**

When violets turn deep **blue**

**C**

Spring rains raise the rose

**B**

The bay mourns its **dew**

**B**

My sock finds its **shoe**

# The Blues

Traditional American blues songs epitomize the most-used rhyme scheme in popular music. Short, simple, easy to remember and sing, the **A A A1** scheme is used in the blues and in other types of popular music as well.

**A**

Sure as I stand here, those roses are **red**

**A**

Sure as I stand here, those roses are **red**

You've done left me,          **A1**
      with my flowers lyin' on your **bed**

Notice that the first two **A** lines are exactly the same. Repeating a line or phrase verbatim can be effective in a pop song in general, and in blues in particular. Notice that the third line is longer than the first two lines.

Another common variation is the **A A A1 A** blues lines, which is also taken literally:

**A**

Sure as I stand here, those roses are **red**

**A**

Sure as I stand here, those roses are **red**

You've done left me,          **A1**
      with my flowers lyin' on your **bed**

                     **A**
Yeah, sure as I stand here, those roses are **red**

# Limerick

## A A B B A

The limerick form in song lyrics has been around in one variation or another since the troubadours of the Middle Ages. And it's still used effectively today. It can add interest when you write the verse in an **A B C B** (or other) form and the chorus as a limerick.

**A**
There once was a rose from **Nantucket**
**A**
That was planted deep in a **bucket**
**B**
Carried to and **fro**
**B**
Always on the **go**
**A**
'Twas happy 'cause no one would **pluck it**

## A A B C C B

A variation on the basic limerick form looks like this:

**A**
His eyes violet **blue**
**A**
And all that I **knew**
**B**
Was that I felt a sense of **wonder**
**C**
His hair auburn **red**
**C**
And what little he **said**
**B**
Was drowned out by the far distant **thunder**

# Triplets

An older, more traditional form of lyric rhyming involves lines of three. It's good to experiment with this form, as it often allows you to expand your horizons musically as well as lyrically. Working out even part of a song with an odd-numbered rhyming scheme (as opposed to the common groups of two or four) can add variety to your material.

## A A A B B B

**A**

The daisies are bright **yellow**

**A**

I'm speaking like **Othello**

**A**

She's moaning like a **cello**

**B**

If I'd have known **sooner**

**B**

She'd be such a **crooner**

**B**

I would've procured me a **tuner**

**A B A B C B (C D C, etc.)**

**A**

I met her in a local **bar**

**B**

She smelled nothing like a **rose**

**A**

Smoking that big fat **cigar**

**B**

And yapping on about her **woes**

**C**

Yet at closin' time, she looked **good**

**B**

Ain't that always how it **goes?**

The scheme possibilities are infinite, limited only by your imagination. It is important to constantly try new combinations of rhyme schemes, to mix and match styles within a song (i.e., a blues-style verse with a limerick chorus), and always avoid that classic beginning songwriter obstacle of allowing all your songs to be structured the same way.

## A Brief History of Rhyme

Poetry originated in the ancient traditions and ceremonies of early tribal societies all over the world. The art of rhyme seems to have been developed by the early Greek and Latin poets, but was more frequently used in medieval religious hymns. Later, poetry broke away from strict religious use and was developed for entertainment purposes.

The rich work of William Shakespeare (1564–1616) used rhyme for comedy and dramatic purposes. It was he who perfected the stanza—and the rhythm of his words and the beautifully haunting and lyrical sounds they create still echo in minds today.

While Shakespeare and his contemporaries used complex rhyming schemes that would probably never find their way into a pop song, it's certainly an exciting place to look for structure ideas and lyric inspiration. The aspiring lyricists who study such work will benefit from it.

### Free Verse

After centuries of strict rules regarding scheme, accent, and rhyme, the American poet Walt Whitman (1819–1892) came along and shook up the poetry world. In 1855, he published a small book of poems entitled *Leaves of Grass*, which had the audacity of not rhyming. This new form was called "free verse." It was also called "trash" and "blasphemous" by many of the established critics of the day (not unlike what they called jazz, then later rock 'n' roll, then later still, rap, when those art forms first appeared on the scene).

At the turn of the century, songs coming out of Tin Pan Alley (a reference to popular songs of the time, usually written in New York) were very strict about rhymes. They were also strict about *meter* (the number of syllables in each line); line by line, they had to match. So there were lots of "moon-spoon-June" songs that, while they rhymed and were certainly good songs, were also restrictive in what they could say, and by the nature of the restrictions, tended to be corny.

By the '60s and '70s, people like Chuck Berry, John Lennon, Bob Dylan, Joni Mitchell, and Mick Jagger (among many others) wrote pop songs that had "near rhymes" or *assonance* in them (words that contained the same vowel sounds but ended in different consonants). This type of evolution happens in every art form: first rules are made, then they're perfected, then they're broken. In this instance, it allowed songwriters more freedom to express their ideas, when expressing ideas was becoming more important than merely coming up with rhymes.

In recent years, people like Adam Duritz (of Counting Crows), Michael Stipe (of R.E.M.), Alanis Morissette, and many others, are writing songs partly in free verse. Meters don't match, lines are erratically short and long, etc., creating a complete poetic breakdown. But this trend allows for the priority to be placed on *what's* being said and less on *how* it's being said.

The most important point is that the idea is expressed, the story is told, and the feeling is conveyed. If you need to tear down the walls of strict rhyme, then do it.

Study the masters. Learn the rules. Then break them and make your own rules, thus creating your own voice.

# The Craft of Lyric Writing

Songwriting is a craft, not just raw talent. Since you have the desire to express your thoughts in song, that already proves you have talent. Now, all you have to do is get better at it.

"I get inspired whenever I work hard," said Igor Stravinsky.

"Genius is 1% inspiration and 99% perspiration," said Thomas Edison.

"Shoo-be doo-be do," said Frank Sinatra, in an infamous recording session when he was so tired he couldn't remember the lyrics that someone had worked so hard to write.

The point is, you'll only get good by doing a lot of lyric writing and by consistently pushing yourself to new limits, and, even then, somebody might forget your words. Never be satisfied with something that's not your best. Always be working on improving a song; then quickly move on and write another. Here's a beginning songwriter's theory: every lyricist has 100 bad songs in them that they have to work out of their system before they start writing any words that are any good. Part of the reason for this is that so many songs by others have seeped into our pores that we're simply regurgitating our musical tastes. That's why it's important to write a lot. It's the only way you'll become a good lyricist.

# 10 Tips to Better Lyric Writing

1. **Save Everything.** Don't throw away any lyrics you write. Keep them in a box, a folder, a file, your sock drawer, wherever—save them even if you immediately dislike them. Later, when you're having a bout of writer's block or just want other ideas, looking through the proverbial junkyard of songs-gone-wrong can be helpful. Even if most of the lyrics are bad, later you may look back and spot one line that was really good—and then want to lift it for your new song. Or you may say, "this is all so bad, but I like the idea of the second verse..." and be able to make it into the chorus of a song that has at this point been chorusless. Or, you may just want to see how far your lyrics have come.

2. **See the Big Picture.** In those moments when you are inspired and can't write the words you hear in your head fast enough, don't get bogged down with the details— always look at the big picture. For example, if you get an idea for the first verse but get stuck halfway through the second verse, don't let yourself lose the feeling by staring at a blank line. Leave it blank and go on to the chorus. Only have one line for the chorus? Fine. Go on to the third verse. Write as much as you can, even if it means leaving holes in your work. When you go to look at it later, maybe finishing the second verse and a chorus will come to you easily...and, meanwhile, you'll have a skeleton frame of a great song to work with.

3. **Analyze Others.** If you like the lyrics of a songwriter, don't just settle for going, "wow—those are great lyrics." Few things in our artistic life happen by accident. Good lyrics certainly don't just happen—they are formed, molded, shaped, and put in a specific order for maximum effect. If the words to a favorite song make you sad, study it—is it painting a picture? Relaying a feeling? Telling a story? How does it do that? Specifically, what line or lines? What about it makes you feel involved? What about it makes you think of something that has happened in your own life? How can you do your own version of that?

Study the work of the masters: Woody Guthrie, Ira Gershwin, Cole Porter, Lawrence Hart, Marvin Gaye, Paul Simon, Mary Chapin-Carpenter, Tori Amos, Elvis Costello, Pete Townshend, Chrissie Hynde, Johnny Cash, and the Beatles, among many others. Live, listen, and learn.

4. **Analyze Yourself.** Develop the necessary ability to look at your work as objectively as possible. Often, people think that everything they do stinks—or that everything they do is great. Chances are, the truth is somewhere in between. Be able to separate yourself from the story or feeling you were trying to convey, and ask yourself: Is this working? What am I trying to say? Am I saying it effectively? Am I trying to say too much? Too little? Learn to distinguish between the good and the bad in your work.

5. **Use Variety.** Search for ways to vary your music in general, and your rhyme schemes in particular. If your verse is A B A B, put your chorus in limerick form; if you have a tendency to write in first person (using "I" and "me"), take the voice of a storyteller; if you always write about yourself, your experiences, and feelings, write about someone you hardly know and whose life is completely different from your own. In the bigger picture, if you always write hard rock, write a love ballad; if you write Broadway-style songs, write a rock song; etc.—if just for the exercise.

6. **Cool Off.** When you write lyrics, you'll probably love them right away. But put them away for a few days—if not a week. Later, with an objective eye, you will be in a better position to fine tune them and spot the song's weaknesses. Don't hesitate to hack at your lyrics, and also have the courage to cut a good line if it's not right for the song.

7. **Avoid Clichés.** After you've written your song and have given yourself a suitable cooling-off period, sit down with it and go over it for what's called the land mines of bad lyric writing—the cliché. If there's even one, it can ruin the song. So if there are any *cuts like a knife, spread your wings and fly, flies like a dove,* or anything else you've heard a billion times, then make yourself say it in a different way—one that's not been heard before. Or, better still, turn the cliché inside out and twist it into something original.

8. **Expand Your Horizons.** Look to other sources for inspiration: the short stories of D. H. Lawrence or James Joyce, the poetry of Robert Frost or Gwendolyn Brooks; the writings of Maya Angelou or even Hunter S. Thompson—or even the art of Picasso or Van Gogh. Obviously you can't recreate what other great artists from other mediums do, but it can make you think in ways that will take you outside your own individual style of lyric writing.

9. **Writer's Block Is No Excuse.** There will be times when you can't think of anything to save your life. Some people think you should wait until the creative muse visits you again and just do nothing until that happens. Others think there can be no excuses: you're a creator, so create. Make yourself write a song—even if what you're writing makes no sense or feels really bad. If you haven't been able to write a song in two months, then make yourself write one a day until you work yourself out of it. Actually, thumbing through this book, just looking at rhymes randomly might be all you need to get you through a dry period.

10. **Show It, Don't Say It.** It's an old saying from the theater, but it also holds true for good lyric writing. Don't say "I felt lonely when you left me" in a song—paint a picture, and show it: "I play a lot of solitaire since you've been gone."

Most of all, keep writing. And keep the faith.

**A**

# A

**Ability**  (see **Be**)

**Able**  cable disable enable fable label sable stable table
unable unstable

**Abolish**  demolish polish tallish

**Abort**  (see **Court**)

**Abortive**  sportive supportive

**About**  boy scout blow-out bout clout devout doubt eke
out flout gout lout out pout roundabout route scout
shout snout spout sprout stout tout trout wash-out
worn-out

**Above**  dove glove ladylove love mourning dove of shove
turtle dove

**Absolute**  (see **Cute**)

**Abstract**  (see **Act**)

**Absurd**  bird blackbird bluebird curd heard herd hummingbird
ladybird mockingbird overheard third word yellowbird

**Abuse**  accuse confuse cues deduce diffuse disuse duce
excuse induce infuse introduce juice misuse obtuse
peruse produce profuse reduce refuse reproduce
seduce Syracuse use

**Abyss**  amiss analysis armistice bliss carcass cowardice dismiss
emphasis hiss hypothesis kiss miss nemesis office
prejudice Swiss synthesis this

**Academic**  endemic epidemic polemic systematic (see *tick*)

**Accelerate**  (see **Ate**)

**Accept**  adept crept except intercept kept overslept slept
stepped swept wept

**Access**  (see **Confess**)

**Account** amount count dismount fount mount
　　　paramount tantamount

**Accuse** (see **Abuse**)

**Ace** base bass brace case chase commonplace debase
　　　disgrace displace embrace encase erase face grace lace
　　　mace misplace pace place race replace space steeplechase
　　　trace unlace vase

**Ache** bake brake break cake fake flake forsake headache
　　　heartache keepsake make mistake opaque quake rake
　　　sake shake snake stake steak take wake

**Achey** flaky quaky shaky snaky

**Achieve** believe bereave conceive disbelieve eve grieve
　　　heave leave perceive receive relieve reprieve retrieve
　　　sleeve weave

**Achievement** bereavement

**Acre** baker breaker dressmaker faker heartbreaker
　　　maker matchmaker pacemaker peacemaker
　　　Quaker shaker strikebreaker taker troublemaker
　　　undertaker watchmaker

**Acrobat** (see **At**)

**Acrobatic** (see **Attic**)

**Across** albatross boss cross double-cross floss gloss loss
　　　moss rhinoceros sauce toss

**Act** abstract attract backed compact contract distract
　　　exact fact impact intact jacked packed pact protract
　　　racked react slacked smacked snacked subtract tact
　　　tracked tract

**Action** abstraction attraction distraction extraction
　　　faction fraction reaction satisfaction subtraction
　　　traction transaction

**Active** attractive extractive inactive proactive
　　　radioactive reactive

A

**Actor**  benefactor contractor detractor distracter
extractor factor reactor refractor tractor

**Actual**  contractual factual

**Ad**  (see **Bad**)

**Add**  (see **Bad**)

**Addict**  conflict constrict contradict convict derelict evict
flicked inflict licked predict pricked strict

**Addiction**  affliction benediction contradiction conviction
crucifixion depiction diction eviction fiction friction
jurisdiction prediction restriction

**Adjourn**  (see **Learn**)

**Adjust**  (see **Trust**)

**Admire**  acquire amplifier aspire attire buyer choir conspire
crier cryer desire dire dryer entire esquire expire fire
flier friar higher hire inquire inspire justifier liar magnifier
multiplier mystifier perspire prior prophesier require
retire satisfier sire squire supplier testifier tire
transpire wire

**Admirer**  direr enquirer hirer inquirer inspirer wirer

**Admission**  (see **Tradition**)

**Adopt**  copped flopped mopped opt popped stopped

**Adventure**  denture indenture misadventure venture

**Advice**  concise device dice entice ice lice mice nice
paradise precise price rice sacrifice spice splice
suffice thrice twice vice

**Advocate**  (see **Ate**)

**Affair**  (see **Air**)

**Affect**  (see **Defect**)

**Affection**  bisection circumspection collection complexion
connection correction defection deflection detection
direction disaffection dissection ejection election erection

imperfection infection inflection inspection intersection
introspection objection perfection projection protection
reflection rejection resurrection retrospection section
selection vivisection

**Afford**  aboard accord award board bored ford harpsichord
hoard lord overboard poured reward shuffleboard soared
sword ward

**Afraid**  aid arcade barricade blade blockade braid brayed
brigade centigrade charade crusade degrade dismayed
dissuade downgrade escapade evade fade grade grenade
hayed invade laid lemonade made maid masquerade paid
parade persuade played promenade raid renegade
serenade shade spade stockade suede tirade trade

**After**  grafter hereafter laughter rafter thereafter

**Afternoon**  (see **Moon**)

**Again**  abstain airplane arraign ascertain attain brain Cain
campaign cane chain champagne cocaine complain contain
crane detain disdain domain drain entertain explain
feign gain grain humane hurricane hydroplane insane
lane main Maine maintain mane migraine obtain ordain
pain pane pertain plain plane profane propane rain refrain
reign rein remain sane slain Spain sprain stain strain
sustain train vain vane vein wane windowpane (see *win*)

**Against**  condensed fenced sensed

**Age**  cage gage page rampage sage stage wage

**Agony**  (see **Be**)

**Agree**  (see **Be**)

**Ailment**  curtailment impalement implement

**Aim**  acclaim became blame came claim exclaim fame flame
frame game inflame lame maim name proclaim same
shame tame

**A**

**Air**  affair anywhere aware bare bear billionaire blare care chair
compare dare debonair declare despair disrepair
elsewhere everywhere fair fare flair glare hair hare heir
impair legionnaire mare midair millionaire nightmare pair
pare pear Pierre prayer prepare rare ready-to-wear repair
scare snare solitaire somewhere spare square stair stare
swear tear their there thoroughfare unaware underwear
unfair ware wear where

**Airplane**  (see **Again**)

**Aisle**  (see **Smile**)

**Alarm**  arm charm disarm farm forearm harm

**Album**  aquarium auditorium become bum burdensome
Christendom come cranium crematorium crumb
curriculum drum dumb emporium fee-fi-fo-fum glum gum
gymnasium hum kettledrum kingdom martyrdom
maximum meddlesome medium millennium minimum
mum museum numb opium overcome pendulum
petroleum platinum plum premium quarrelsome radium
random rum sanitarium scum slum some strum succumb
sum swum tedium thumb Tom Thumb Tweedledum
uranium worrisome yum

**Ale**  bail bale blackmail braille cocktail curtail exhale fail female
flail frail hail hale impale inhale jail mail male nail pale
prevail rail regale sail sale scale shale snail stale tail they'll
veil whale

**Alert**  (see **Hurt**)

**Alibi**  (see **Cry**)

**Alien**  Australian Episcopalian

**Alimony**  acrimony baloney bony crony macaroni matrimony
patrimony phony pony sanctimony stony testimony Tony

**All**  ball bawl brawl call crawl doll drawl enthrall fall gall haul
install mall maul Montreal nightfall overhaul parasol pitfall
protocol rainfall scrawl shawl small snowfall sprawl stall
tall thrall wall waterfall y'all

**Allege**  dredge edge fledge hedge ledge privilege sacrilege
sledge wedge

**Alley**  dilly-dally rally Sally tally valley

**Allow**  avow bough bow brow chow cow disavow endow frau
how kowtow now ow plough plow row slough somehow
sow thou vow wow

**Allude**  (see **Feud**)

**Allure**  (see **Cure**)

**Almighty**  Aphrodite flighty mightily righty

**Alone**  atone backbone baritone blown bone chaperone
clone condone cone cornerstone cyclone Dictaphone
flown full-blown full-grown gramophone grindstone
groan grown headstone known loan lone microphone
milestone moan monotone mown overgrown overthrown
own phone postpone prone saxophone sewn shown
stone telephone thrown tone trombone unknown
xylophone zone

**Along**  belong bong ding-dong gong Hong Kong long
ping-pong prong song strong throng wrong

**Altar**  alter defaulter falter Gibraltar halter Psalter

**Always**  hallways small ways (see *way*)

**Am**  Amsterdam anagram Birmingham cam clam cram dam
damn diaphragm gram ham jam lamb ma'am madame
scram sham slam swam telegram tram yam

**Amateur**  (see **Her**)

**Amaze**  ablaze appraise bays blaze braze craze days daze faze
gaze glaze graze haze malaise mayonnaise maze nays
nowadays plays polonaise praise ways

**A**

**Amble**  gamble ramble scramble shamble

**Amen**  citizen den fen hen hydrogen Ken men oxygen pen
regimen specimen ten then yen Zen

**Among**  (see **Young**)

**Amorous**  clamorous glamorous (see *us*)

**Amount**  account count dismount fount mount
paramount tantamount

**Amp**  camp champ clamp cramp damp lamp ramp stamp vamp

**Analysis**  catalysis dialysis paralysis (see *miss*)

**Anchor**  banker canker flanker franker rancor ranker
spanker tanker thank 'er

**And**  band brand canned command contraband demand
expand fanned grand hand land panned planned
reprimand Rio Grande sand stand

**Angelic**  relic

**Angle**  dangle entangle jangle mangle spangle strangle tangle
triangle wrangle

**Anguish**  languish

**Anniversary**  cursory nursery (see **Be**)

**Annoy**  (see **Boy**)

**Annual**  manual

**Another**  brother mother other smother

**Ant**  aunt can't chant decant enchant grant implant plant rant
scant shan't slant transplant

**Anxiety**  (see **Be**)

**Anxiety**  impropriety notoriety piety propriety sobriety
society variety

**Any**  Benny Jenny many penny

**Anyone**  anyone begun bun comparison done everyone fun
Galveston gun hon Hun jettison none nun oblivion one
outdone outrun overdone overrun phenomenon pun

run shun simpleton skeleton son stun sun ton unison
venison won

**Anything**  (see **Sing**)

**Apart**  art cart chart counterpart dart depart heart mart part
smart start sweetheart tart upstart

**Ape**  cape cityscape drape escape grape landscape seascape
shape tape

**Apologize**  (see **Lies**)

**Apostle**  colossal docile fossil jostle

**Appalled**  bald scald

**Appear**  (see **Near**)

**Appearance**  adherence clearance coherence disappearance
incoherence interference perseverance

**Applaud**  abroad awed broad clod cod defraud façade fraud
God guffawed Izod nod odd pod prod promenade quad
rod roughshod shod sod squad trod wad

**Applauding**  defrauding lauding marauding plodding prodding

**Applause**  because cause clause claws gauze laws menopause
Oz pause paws Santa Claus was

**Apple**  chapel dapple grapple scrapple

**Appliance**  alliance compliance defiance reliance

**Appreciate**  (see **Ate**)

**Apprehensive**  comprehensive defensive expensive extensive
incomprehensive inexpensive intensive offensive pensive

**Approach**  broach coach cockroach encroach poach
reproach roach

**Approve**  behoove disapprove disprove groove improve move
prove remove

**Arbor**  barber harbor (see *door*)

**Arcade**  (see **Afraid**)

**Arch**  march parch starch

**A**

**Are**   bar bazaar bizarre car caviar cigar Czar disbar far guitar jar par scar sitar spar star tar

**Area**   Bulgaria malaria

**Arena**   Athena concertina hyena Messina subpoena Tina

**Argument**   (see **Bent**)

**Aristocrat**   (see **At**)

**Aristocratic**   (see **Attic**)

**Ark**   aardvark arc bark dark embark hark lark mark narc park patriarch remark shark spark stark

**Arm**   alarm charm disarm farm forearm harm

**Aroma**   coma diploma sarcoma Sonoma Tacoma

**Around**   (see **Found**)

**Arrange**   change derange estrange exchange range strange

**Arrow**   barrow harrow marrow narrow sparrow tarot

**Art**   apart cart chart counterpart dart depart heart mart part smart start sweetheart tart upstart

**Article**   particle

**Artificial**   beneficial initial judicial official sacrificial superficial

**Artisan**   partisan

**Ash**   balderdash bash brash cash clash crash dash flash gnash lash mash rash rehash slash smash splash stash thrash trash

**Ask**   bask cask flask mask masque task

**Asp**   clasp gasp grasp

**Ass**   (see **Class**)

**Assault**   cobalt exalt fault halt malt salt somersault vault

**Assistant**   consistent distant existent inconsistent insistent persistent resistant subsistent

**Asteroid**   avoid alkaloid joyed Lloyd Sigmund Freud tabloid toyed void

**At**   acrobat aristocrat autocrat bat brat bureaucrat cat chat democrat diplomat drat fat flat gnat hat mat pat rat rat-a-tat-tat sat scat spat stat thermostat vat

**Ate**  *one syllable:*
bait crate date eight hate late mate plate rate skate slate
state straight strait trait wait weight

*two syllable:*
await berate debate dictate donate equate estate
frustrate irate locate narrate ornate placate relate rotate
sedate translate vacate

*three syllable:*
abdicate advocate aggravate agitate amputate animate
annotate arbitrate assimilate calculate candidate captivate
celebrate circulate compensate complicate concentrate
confiscate congratulate consecrate consolidate constipate
consummate contaminate contemplate cooperate
coordinate correlate culminate cultivate decimate
decorate dedicate demonstrate desecrate designate
detonate devastate dislocate dissipate dominate duplicate
educate elevate estimate excavate fabricate fascinate
fluctuate formulate generate graduate gravitate habituate
heavyweight hesitate hibernate illustrate imitate implicate
incubate innovate inordinate insulate isolate lacerate
legislate levitate liberate liquidate lubricate magistrate
marinate mediate moderate modulate motivate nominate
operate orchestrate oscillate overate overstate
overweight penetrate perpetrate populate punctuate
radiate regulate reinstate renovate ruminate saturate
second-rate separate simulate situate speculate stimulate
stipulate suffocate tabulate terminate titillate tolerate
underrate understate underweight vacillate validate
vegetate ventilate vindicate violate

**A**

*four or more syllable:*
accelerate accentuate accommodate accumulate affiliate
alienate annihilate appreciate appropriate articulate
assassinate associate collaborate commemorate
commiserate communicate conciliate corroborate
decapitate deliberate depreciate deteriorate discriminate
elaborate eliminate emancipate emulate enunciate
eradicate evacuate evaluate evaporate excommunicate
exonerate extenuate exterminate facilitate humiliate
illuminate incapacitate incarcerate incorporate incriminate
inculcate infatuate impersonate insinuate intimidate
intoxicate invigorate manipulate necessitate negotiate
obliterate originate participate pontificate precipitate
procrastinate reciprocate regurgitate rehabilitate
reiterate rejuvenate resuscitate retaliate reverberate
subordinate (see *deviate*)

**Athlete** (see **Sweet**)

**Athletic** aesthetic alphabetic apathetic apologetic arithmetic
cosmetic electromagnetic energetic frenetic genetic
pathetic poetic sympathetic synthetic theoretic

**Atlantis** mantis

**Atomic** anatomic comic economic

**Attach** batch catch detach dispatch hatch latch match patch
scratch snatch

**Attack** (see **Back**)

**Attempt** contempt dreamt exempt tempt unkempt

**Attend** (see **Friend**)

**Attention** abstention apprehension ascension
comprehension condescension convention dissension
detention dimension dissension extension intention
intervention invention mention retention
suspension tension

**A**

**Attentive**  inattentive incentive inventive retentive

**Attic**  acrobatic aristocratic aromatic autocratic bureaucratic
chromatic cinematic climatic democratic dogmatic
dramatic erratic fanatic melodramatic operatic pragmatic
problematic static stigmatic systematic thematic traumatic

**Attitude**  gratitude latitude platitude

**Attorney**  journey tourney (see *be*)

**Attractive**  active extractive inactive proactive
radioactive reactive

**Audition**  (see **Tradition**)

**Aura**  angora aurora flora Nora sinora Torah

**Autumn**  bottom

**Avenue**  (see **Knew**)

**Avoid**  alkaloid asteroid joyed Lloyd Sigmund Freud
tabloid toyed void

**Award**  (see **Lord**)

**Aware**  (see **Air**)

**Awe**  Arkansas awe bra caw claw draw flaw gnaw guffaw
hurrah jaw law Ma macaw nah overdraw Pa paw raw
saw seesaw shah slaw squaw straw thaw withdraw

**Awesome**  blossom possum (see *some*)

**Awful**  lawful

**Awhile**  (see **Smile**)

**Ax**  backs fax jacks lax max relax packs Saks sax slacks tax wax

# B

**Babble**  dabble rabble scrabble

**Baby**  maybe (see *be*)

**Bachelor**  (see **Door**)

**Back**  almanac attack black bric-a-brac Cadillac cardiac
clickety-clack egomaniac feedback hack Hackensack
haystack jack kleptomaniac knack lack maniac pack plaque
Pontiac prozac quack rack sack shack slack snack stack
tack track whack yak zodiac

**Bacon**  (see **Taken**)

**Bad**  ad add Brad cad Chad clad Dad egad fad glad grad had
lad nomad pad plaid sad shad Trinidad

**Baffle**  raffle snaffle

**Bag**  brag drag flag gag hag lag mag nag rag sag shag slag snag
stag swag tag wag

**Bait**  (see **Ate**)

**Balcony**  (see **Be**)

**Bald**  appalled scald

**Ball**  all bawl brawl call crawl doll drawl fall gall haul install mall
maul Montreal nightfall overhaul parasol pitfall protocol
rainfall scrawl shawl small snowfall sprawl stall tall thrall
wall waterfall y'all

**Ballad**  invalid salad valid

**Balloon**  (see **Moon**)

**Banana**  (see **Nirvana**)

**Band**  and bland brand canned command contraband demand
expand fanned grand hand land panned planned
reprimand Rio Grande sand stand

**Bandstand**  grandstand handstand

**Bang**　boomerang clang dang fang orangutan rang sang
　　　slang sprang

**B**

**Bank**　blank clank crank dank drank flank frank hank
　　　outrank plank prank rank sank shrank spank stank
　　　tank thank yank

**Banker**　anchor canker flanker franker rancor ranker spanker
　　　tanker thank 'er

**Bar**　bazaar bizarre car caviar cigar Czar disbar far guitar jar
　　　par scar spar star tar

**Barb**　garb

**Barber**　arbor harbor (see *door*)

**Barf**　scarf snarf

**Barge**　charge discharge enlarge large

**Bark**　aardvark arc ark dark embark hark lark mark narc park
　　　patriarch remark shark spark stark

**Barn**　darn yarn

**Barracuda**　Bermuda Buddha gouda

**Barrage**　camouflage garage entourage mirage

**Barrel**　apparel carol

**Barrier**　carrier terrier (see *her*)

**Base**　(see **Ace**)

**Bash**　ash balderdash brash cash clash crash dash flash
　　　gnash lash mash rash rehash slash smash splash
　　　stash thrash trash

**Basket**　casket gasket (see *it, get*)

**Baste**　aftertaste braced chaste distaste faced freckle-faced
　　　haste hatchet-faced lambaste paste taste two-faced
　　　waist waste

**Bat**　(see **At**)

**Batch**　attach catch detach dispatch hatch latch match
　　　patch scratch snatch

**Bath**  aftermath homeopath math path psychopath
sociopath wrath

**B**

**Battery**  flattery (see *be*)

**Battle**  cattle chattel embattle prattle rattle Seattle tattle

**Bay**  (see **Say**)

**Be**  *one syllable:*
bee fee flea flee free gee glee he key knee me plea pea
sea see she tea thee tree we wee ye

*two syllable:*
agree debris decree degree foresee goatee Gumby
hee-hee Marie R&D theory trustee wintry

*three syllable:*
absentee agency agony amnesty ancestry archery armory
artistry bakery balcony battery bigotry blasphemy botany
bourgeoisie bravery brevity bribery burglary Calgary
calvary casualty cavity century certainty charity chastity
chickadee chimpanzee chivalry clemency colony comedy
company courtesy crudity cruelty custody decency
deputy destiny devotee diary dignity disagree DMZ
drapery dynasty ebony ecstasy effigy elegy embassy
employee enemy energy eulogy factory fallacy family
fantasy felony fertility fiery first-degree flagrancy flattery
fluency forgery frequency gaiety galaxy Galilee gallantry
gallery Germany gravity guarantee harmony heresy
hierarchy history homily honesty imagery industry infamy
infancy infantry injury inquiry irony Italy ivory jamboree
jealousy jeopardy jewelry jubilee legacy leniency levity
liberty liturgy lottery loyalty lunacy luxury melody
memory mercury mimicry ministry misery mockery
modesty mutiny mystery nominee nursery odyssey

oversee pageantry papacy parody paternity pedantry
pedigree penalty perjury Ph.D. piety piracy pleasantry
poetry poignancy policy potpourri poverty privacy
prodigy property puberty purity quackery quality quantity
rarity recipe rectory referee refugee remedy repartee
revelry rhapsody rickety rivalry robbery rosemary royalty
salary sanctity sanity savagery savory scarcity scenery
scrutiny secrecy sesame shadowy shivery silvery simile
slavery slippery sorcery strategy subsidy subtlety sugary
summary symmetry sympathy symphony tapestry
tendency Tennessee thievery timpani treachery trickery
trilogy trinity truancy tyranny unity urgency victory
watery witchery

*four or more syllable:*
ability absurdity activity actuality adversity affinity agility
ambiguity amenity animosity anarchy anatomy anniversary
anonymity antiquity anxiety artillery astrology astronomy
atrocity audacity authenticity authority barbarity
biography biology brilliancy brutality capacity
captivity celebrity Christianity chronology combustibility
commodity community compatibility complacency
complexity complimentary comprehensibility conformity
consistency conspiracy contradictory criminality curiosity
debauchery deformity delivery dependency depravity
diversity diplomacy directory discovery discrepancy
divinity eccentricity economy efficiency electricity
elementary emergency enormity epitome equality
eternity expectancy extremity facility facsimile ferocity
festivity fiddle-de-dee fidelity formality fraternity frivolity
futility generosity geography geometry gratuity heredity
hilarity hospitably hostility humanity humility hypocrisy

**B**

identity idiocy illiteracy immodesty immunity inability
incapacity inconsistency indecency individuality inferiority
infirmary infirmity ingenuity inhumanity insufficiency
insurgency integrity intensity legality longevity machinery
mahogany majesty maternity maturity mediocrity minority
mobility monogamy monopoly monstrosity morality
mythology nationality nativity necessity neutrality nobility
notoriety peculiarity personality philanthropy philosophy
photography popularity pornography posterity prosperity
priority profanity proficiency promiscuity propriety
proximity psychiatry publicity reality recovery
rudimentary satisfactory security sensibility sensuality
sentimentality serenity severity sexuality similarity
simplicity sincerity society sophistry spontaneity
stability sterility stupidity subjectively superficiality
superiority technicality theology totality tranquillity
triviality uniformity university utility validity variety
velocity virginity vulgarity

**Beach**  breach each impeach leech peach preach reach
screech speech teach

**Bean**  (see **Mean**)

**Beard**  appeared cleared disappeared feared jeered neared
persevered smeared speared weird

**Beast**  ceased creased deceased east feast least pieced
priest yeast

**Beat**  athlete beet bittersweet bleat cheat compete complete
conceit concrete deceit defeat delete deplete discreet
discrete eat elite feat feet fleet greet heat incomplete
indiscreet meat meet mistreat neat obsolete parakeet
receipt repeat retreat seat sheet sleet street suite sweet
treat wheat

**Beaten**  cheatin' Cretan eaten Eton meetin'
    sweeten unbeaten

**B**

**Beautiful**  dutiful full (see *wool*)

**Beauty**  cutie duty

**Became**  (see **Aim**)

**Because**  applause cause clause claws gauze laws menopause
    Oz pause paws Santa Claus was

**Become**  (see **Dumb**)

**Bed**  ahead bedspread bread bred coed dead dread fed
    figurehead fled flowerbed fountainhead gingerbread head
    inbred lead led misled misread overfed read red riverbed
    said shed shred sled sped spread thoroughbred thread
    underfed unthread wed

**Beef**  belief brief chief disbelief grief leaf reef relief thief

**Been**  again aspirin begin Berlin bin chagrin chin discipline
    feminine fin genuine gin grin harlequin heroine in inn kin
    mandolin mannequin masculine moccasin origin pin
    saccharine shin sin skin spin thick-and-thin thin tin twin
    violin win within

**Beer**  adhere appear atmosphere auctioneer bombardier
    career cashier cavalier chandelier cheer clear dear
    deer disappear ear engineer fear financier frontier gear
    hear hemisphere here insincere interfere jeer lavaliere
    leer mere mountaineer near overhear overseer peer
    persevere pioneer queer racketeer reappear rear revere
    seer severe shear sheer sincere smear sneer spear sphere
    stratosphere tear veneer volunteer year

**B**

**Before** abhor ambassador ashore auditor bachelor Baltimore boar bore chancellor chore commodore competitor conspirator contributor core corps corridor deplore dinosaur door drawer Ecuador editor emperor encore evermore explore exterior floor folklore for fore four furthermore galore governor ignore implore inferior lore matador metaphor more nevermore nor oar offshore or orator ore poor pour rapport restore roar score seashore senator señor shore Singapore snore soar sophomore sore spore store swore therefore Thor tore troubadour underscore uproar visitor yore your

**Beg** egg keg leg peg

**Begin** again aspirin been Berlin bin chagrin chin discipline feminine fin genuine gin grin harlequin heroine in inn kin mandolin mannequin masculine moccasin origin pin saccharine shin sin skin spin thick-and-thin thin tin twin violin win within

**Beginner** B. F. Skinner breadwinner dinner inner sinner skinner spinner thinner winner

**Begun** anyone bun comparison everyone fun Galveston gun hon Hun jettison none nun oblivion one outdone outrun overdone overrun phenomenon pun run shun simpleton skeleton son stun sun ton unison venison won

**Behavior** misbehavior savior

**Being** agreeing decreeing disagreeing farseeing fleeing foreseeing freeing guaranteeing overseeing seeing teeing unseeing

**Belch** squelch welch

**Belief** beef brief chief disbelief grief leaf relief thief

**Believe**  achieve bereave conceive disbelieve eve grieve
　　　　heave leave perceive receive relieve reprieve retrieve
　　　　sleeve weave

**Bell**  belle caramel Carmel carrousel cell clientele dell dwell
　　　excel farewell fell gel hell hotel infidel knell mademoiselle
　　　personnel sell shell smell spell tell well yell

**Belly**  deli jelly Kelly Shelly smelly

**Belong**  along belong bong ding-dong gong Hong Kong long
　　　　Ping-Pong prong song strong throng wrong

**Below**  (see **Blow**)

**Belt**  Celt dealt felt heartfelt melt pelt welt

**Bench**  clench drench French monkey wrench quench stench
　　　trench wench wrench

**Bend**  (see **Friend**)

**Beneath**  heath teeth underneath wreath

**Beneficial**  artificial initial judicial official sacrificial superficial

**Benevolent**  malevolent

**Bent**  *one syllable:*
　　　cent dent gent Lent lent rent sent spent tent vent went

　　　*two syllable:*
　　　accent assent cement comment convent consent content
　　　descent diment event ferment fluent frequent invent
　　　meant percent present prevent relent repent resent
　　　torment unbent well-meant

　　　*three syllable:*
　　　accident affluent acedent president prominent
　　　punishment regiment represent resident reverent
　　　sacrament sediment sentiment settlement subsequent
　　　succulent supplement temperament tenement testament
　　　tournament violent wonderment

*four or more syllable:*

abandonment acknowledgment advertisement benevolent bewilderment coincident development disarmament embarrassment embellishment embezzlement embodiment encouragement enlightenment environment establishment experiment imprisonment incompetent ingredient intelligent intent invent irreverent malevolent misrepresent predicament replenishment self-confident

**Best**  arrest attest blessed breast Bucharest Budapest celeste chest congest contest crest detest digest divest dressed guessed guest infest ingest interest invest jest manifest messed molest nest pest protest request rest second-best suggest test unrest vest zest

**Bet**  (see **Met**)

**Bethlehem**  condemn gem hem phlegm requiem stem them

**Better**  debtor getter letter setter sweater wetter (see *her*)

**Beyond**  blond bond correspond dawned fond pond respond spawned vagabond wand yawned

**Bible**  libel tribal

**Bicycle**  icicle tricycle

**Bid**  did forbid grid hid invalid lid Madrid pyramid rid skid slid squid

**Big**  dig fig gig jig pig rig swig thingamajig twig wig

**Bigot**  spigot

**Bike**  hike like mike spike strike tyke

**Biker**  hiker piker spiker striker (see *her*)

**Bill**  (see **Fill**)

**Bingo**  dingo flamingo gringo jingo lingo (see *glow*)

**Bird**  absurd blackbird bluebird curd heard herd hummingbird
ladybird mockingbird overheard third word yellowbird

**Birth**  dearth earth girth mirth worth

**Biscuit**  brisket (see *it*)

**Bitch**  bewitch ditch enrich glitch hitch pitch rich snitch stitch
switch twitch which

**Bite**  (see **Night**)

**Bitter**  counterfeiter critter fitter fritter glitter litter quitter
sitter transmitter twitter (see *her*)

**Bizarre**  are bar bazaar car caviar cigar Czar disbar far guitar
jar par scar spar star tar

**Blab**  cab crab dab drab gab grab jab lab nab scab slab stab tab

**Blade**  (see **Afraid**)

**Blame**  acclaim aim became came claim exclaim fame
flame frame game inflame lame maim name proclaim
same shame tame

**Blank**  bank clank crank dank drank flank frank hank
outrank plank prank rank sank shrank spank stank tank
thank yank

**Blast**  aghast cast classed contrast fast flabbergast forecast
gassed last mast outlast overcast passed past vast

**Blatant**  latent patent

**Blaze**  ablaze amaze appraise bays braze craze days daze faze
gaze glaze graze haze malaise mayonnaise maze nays
nowadays plays polonaise praise ways

**Blazer**  appraiser gazer laser maser phaser praiser
razor stargazer

**B**

**B**

**Bleed**  agreed breed centipede concede creed deed exceed
feed greed heed inbreed knead lead mislead need precede
proceed read recede reed secede seed speed stampede
succeed Swede tweed weed

**Blemish**  Flemish

**Blend**  (see **Friend**)

**Bless**  (see **Confess**)

**Blind**  behind bind find grind hind humankind kind mastermind
mind remind signed unkind unwind wind wined

**Blinded**  evil-minded feebleminded like-minded minded
narrow-minded reminded

**Blink**  brink chink clink drink fink ink kink link mink pink rink
shrink sink slink stink think wink zinc

**Bliss**  abyss amiss analysis armistice carcass cowardice dismiss
emphasis hiss hypothesis kiss miss nemesis office
prejudice Swiss synthesis this

**Blister**  assister magister mister resister sister
twister (see *her*)

**Blizzard**  gizzard lizard scissored wizard

**Bloat**  (see **Boat**)

**Blond**  (see **Beyond**)

**Blood**  bud cud dud flood mud scud spud stud thud

**Bloom**  boom broom cloakroom doom entomb flume gloom
groom room tomb whom womb zoom

**Blossom**  awesome possum (see *some*)

**Blouse**  douse grouse house louse madhouse mouse outhouse
penthouse slaughterhouse souse spouse

**Blow**  afro although banjo beau below bestow bow buffalo
bungalow calico crossbow crow depot doe domino dough
embryo escrow Eskimo flow foe forgo fro gazebo gigolo
glow go grow heigh-ho ho-ho hobo hoe incognito
indigo Joe know long ago low Mexico mistletoe mow no

oboe oh outgrow overflow overgrow overthrow owe
Pinocchio pistachio plateau quo rainbow ratio roe row
sew slow snow so Soho status quo stow studio tally-ho
though throw tiptoe to-and-fro toe Tokyo tow tremolo
undergo undertow vertigo woe yo yo-yo

**Blown**  (see **Known**)

**Blue**  (see **Do**)

**Blues**  booze bruise choose cruise lose news ooze
snooze whose

**Bluff**  buff cuff duff enough fluff gruff huff muff powder puff
rough scruff scuff snuff stuff tough

**Blunder**  plunder under thunder wonder

**Blunt**  affront bunt confront forefront front grunt hunt punt
runt shunt stunt

**Blur**  (see **Her**)

**Board**  (see **Lord**)

**Boast**  coast foremost furthermost ghost host innermost
most post roast toast whipping post

**Boat**  afloat antidote bloat coat connote denote dote float
footnote gloat goat misquote moat note oat overcoat
promote quote remote riverboat rote smote throat tote
underwrote vote wrote

**Body**  embody gaudy lawdy nobody shoddy somebody toddy

**Bold**  behold blindfold centerfold cold fold foothold foretold
gold hold household marigold mold old retold scold sold
told uphold withhold

**Bolt**  colt dolt jolt revolt thunderbolt

**Bomb**  aplomb calm embalm Guam Mom palm psalm qualm

**Bombard**  avant-garde card chard discard disregard guard
hard lard regard retard tarred yard

**Bomber**  calmer embalmer palmer (see *her*)

**B**

**Bond**  beyond blond correspond fond dawned pond respond
spawned vagabond wand yawned

**Bone**  (see **Known**)

**Book**  brook cook crook hook look mistook nook outlook
rook shook took undertook

**Boom**  bloom broom cloakroom doom entomb flume gloom
groom room tomb whom womb zoom

**Boost**  roost

**Booth**  couth Duluth sleuth tooth truth uncouth youth

**Booty**  cootie fruity snooty tutti-frutti

**Booze**  blues bruise choose cruise lose news ooze
snooze whose

**Boozer**  accuser amuser cruiser lose 'er loser muser oozer
refuser snoozer user (see *her*)

**Border**  boarder disorder hoarder order recorder

**Born**  adorn airborne Cape Horn Capricorn corn horn
lovelorn Matterhorn morn mourn popcorn scorn
stillborn sworn unicorn warn worn

**Borrow**  morrow sorrow tomorrow

**Botch**  blotch crotch debauch hopscotch notch Scotch
watch wristwatch

**Both**  growth loath oath overgrowth undergrowth

**Bottle**  dottle mottle throttle waddle wattle

**Bottom**  autumn

**Bought**  astronaut brought caught cosmonaut fought naught
ought overwrought sought taught thought wrought

**Bounce**  announce counts denounce mounts ounce pounce
pronounce renounce trounce

**Bound**  (see **Found**)

**Boundary**  foundry

**B**

**Bout**  about boy scout blow-out clout devout doubt eke out flout gout lout out pout roundabout route scout shout snout spout sprout stout tout trout wash-out worn-out

**Bow**  (see **Blow**)

**Bowl**  (see **Control**)

**Box**  chickenpox equinox fox mailbox orthodox ox paradox socks stocks rocks Xerox

**Boy**  ahoy annoy buoy convoy corduroy coy decoy destroy employ enjoy Illinois joy ploy Roy Savoy soy toy troy viceroy

**Brag**  bag drag flag gag hag lag mag nag rag sag shag slag snag stag swag tag wag

**Bragger**  bagger carpet-bagger dagger stagger swagger tagger

**Brain**  (see **Chain**)

**Branch**  avalanche ranch

**Brand**  and band canned command contraband demand expand fanned grand hand land panned planned reprimand Rio Grande sand stand

**Brandy**  Andy candy dandy handy randy sandy

**Brass**  (see **Class**)

**Brat**  (see **At**)

**Brave**  behave cave concave crave engrave forgave gave grave knave pave rave save shave slave waive wave

**Bravery**  savory slavery

**Bread**  ahead bed bedspread bred coed dead dread fed figurehead fled flowerbed fountainhead gingerbread head inbred lead led misled misread overfed read red riverbed said shed shred sled sped spread thoroughbred thread underfed unthread wed

**Breadline**  headline deadline

**B**

**Break**  ache bake brake cake fake flake forsake headache
heartache keepsake make mistake opaque quake rake
sake shake snake stake steak take wake

**Breakup**  make-up shake-up take up wake up

**Breath**  death Macbeth

**Breather**  either neither

**Breathing**  seething teething

**Bribe**  circumscribe describe jibe prescribe scribe
subscribe tribe

**Brick**  arithmetic arsenic candlestick candlewick Catholic chick
click flick heartsick hick kick lick limerick love-sick lunatic
maverick nick pick sick slick stick thick tic tick wick

**Bride**  beside bonafide collide confide countryside decide
defied died dignified divide eyed fireside guide hide hillside
homicide inside lied outside override pride provide reside
ride side slide snide stride subdivide subside suicide tide
tried wide yuletide

**Bridge**  abridge fridge ridge

**Bright**  (see **Flight**)

**Brilliant**  resilient

**Bring**  (see **Sing**)

**Broke**  artichoke baroque bloke choke cloak coke croak evoke
folk invoke joke oak poke provoke revoke smoke soak
spoke stroke toke woke yoke

**Broth**  cloth froth moth swath wroth

**Brother**  another mother other smother

**Brought**  (see **Thought**)

**Brown**  clown crown down downtown drown frown gown
hand-me-down noun renown town tumble-down upside
down uptown

**Brunch**  bunch crunch hunch lunch munch punch scrunch

**Brush**  blush crush flush gush lush mush plush rush slush
     thrush underbrush

**B**

**Brute**  (see **Cute**)

**Bubble**  double rubble stubble trouble

**Buck**  (see **Truck**)

**Bucket**  Nantucket (see *it*)

**Buckle**  arbuckle chuckle honeysuckle knuckle suckle

**Budge**  drudge fudge grudge judge misjudge nudge smudge

**Buff**  (see **Bluff**)

**Bug**  drug dug jug hug lug mug plug pug rug shrug slug smug
     snug thug tug

**Bugle**  frugal fugal

**Build**  chilled drilled filled guild killed rebuild willed

**Builder**  bewilder (see *her*)

**Built**  guilt hilt jilt kilt quilt spilt stilt tilt Vanderbilt wilt

**Bulge**  divulge indulge

**Bull**  cock-and-bull do-able full pull wool (see *beautiful*)

**Bum**  (see **Dumb**)

**Bump**  chump clump dump hump jump lump plump rump
     slump stump thump trump ump

**Bunch**  brunch crunch hunch lunch munch punch scrunch

**Bungle**  jungle

**Bunny**  funny honey sunny

**Burial**  aerial

**Burn**  adjourn churn concern discern earn fern intern
     kern learn overturn return sojourn spurn stern
     taciturn turn urn yearn

**Burnt**  learnt weren't

**Burp**  chirp twirp usurp Wyatt Earp

**Burrow**  borough furrow thorough

**Burst**  cursed first nursed outburst thirst versed worst

**B**

**Bury**  (see **Cherry**)

**Bus**  (see **Us**)

**Bush**  cush push

**Bust**  (see **Trust**)

**Bustle**  corpuscle hustle muscle mussel rustle tussle

**Busy**  dizzy frizzy Lizzie tin lizzie tizzy

**But**  butt cut glut gut halibut hut King Tut mutt nut putt rut
scuttlebutt shut smut strut uncut

**Butler**  scuttler subtler

**Butter**  clutter cutter flutter gutter mutter putter shutter
sputter strutter stutter utter

**Button**  cuttin' glutton guttin' mutton nuthin'

**Buzz**  abuzz buzz cause coz does fuzz was

**By**  (see **Bye**)

**Bye**  alibi amplify banzai barfly butterfly buy by certify clarify
crucify cry defy deify deny die dignify diversify dragonfly
drive-by dry dye eye firefly fly fry glorify gratify guy high
horrify I identify imply July justify lie lullaby modify my
mystify notify passerby pie pry qualify rely rye satisfy
sci-fi shy sigh signify simplify sky sly specify spry spy
terrify testify thigh tie try underlie verify why

# C

**Cab**  blab crab dab drab gab grab jab lab nab scab slab stab tab

**Cable**  (see **Able**)

**Cad**  (see **Bad**)

**Cage**  age gage page rampage sage stage wage

**Calf**  carafe epitaph giraffe graph paragraph phonograph
photograph polygraph  riffraff  staff telegraph

**Call**  all ball bawl brawl crawl doll drawl fall gall haul install mall
maul Montreal nightfall overhaul parasol pitfall protocol
rainfall scrawl shawl small snowfall sprawl stall tall thrall
wall waterfall y'all

**Calm**  aplomb bomb CD-ROM embalm Guam Mom palm
psalm qualm

**Calmer**  bomber embalmer palmer

**Calorie**  gallery Mallory salary

**Camp**  amp champ clamp cramp damp lamp ramp stamp vamp

**Can**  ban can-can Dan fan Iran man Nan plan ran Tehran

**Can't**  ant aunt chant decant enchant grant implant plant rant
scant shan't slant transplant

**Canal**  chorale gal morale pal shall

**Canary**  (see **Cherry**)

**Candidate**  (see **Ate**)

**Candle**  dandle handle sandal scandal vandal

**Candy**  Andy brandy dandy handy randy sandy

**Cap**  chap clap flap gap handicap lap map mishap nap rap sap
scrap slap snap strap tap trap wrap zap

**Cape**  ape cityscape drape escape grape landscape seascape
shape tape

**Captive**  adaptive (see *active*)

**Captivity** (see **Be**)

**Capture** rapture recapture (see *your*)

**Car** are bar bazaar bizarre caviar cigar czar disbar far guitar jar par scar spar star tar

**Carat** carrot parrot

**Card** avant-garde bombard card discard disregard guard hard lard regard retard tarred yard

**Care** affair air anywhere aware bare bear billionaire blare chair compare dare debonair declare despair disrepair elsewhere everywhere fair fare flair glare hair hare heir impair legionnaire mare midair millionaire nightmare pair pare pear Pierre prayer prepare rare ready-to-wear repair scare snare solitaire somewhere spare square stair stare swear tear their there thoroughfare unaware underwear unfair ware wear where

**Career** (see **Near**)

**Cargo** argot embargo Fargo largo

**Carol** apparel barrel

**Carp** harp sharp

**Carriage** disparage marriage miscarriage

**Carry** hari-kari marry miscarry parry vary (see *cherry*)

**Cart** apart art chart counterpart dart depart heart mart part smart start sweetheart tart upstart

**Cartoon** (see **Moon**)

**Carve** starve

**Case** (see **Ace**)

**Cash** ash balderdash bash brash clash crash dash flash gnash rash rehash slash smash splash stash thrash trash

**Casino** andantino bambino Filipino keno Reno

**Cask** ask bask flask mask masque task

**Casket** basket gasket (see *it, get*)

**Cast**  aghast blast classed contrast fast flabbergast forecast
gassed last mast outlast overcast passed past vast

**Castle**  tassel vassal wrassle

**Casualty**  (see **Be**)

**Cat**  (see **At**)

**Catch**  attach batch detach dispatch hatch latch match
patch scratch snatch

**Catch**  etch fetch kvetch retch sketch stretch wretch

**Catcher**  dispatcher scratcher snatcher

**Catholic**  (see **Brick**)

**Cattle**  battle chattel embattle prattle rattle Seattle tattle

**Caught**  astronaut bought brought cosmonaut fought naught
ought overwrought sought taught thought wrought

**Cause**  applause because clause claws gauze laws menopause
Oz pause paws Santa Claus was

**Cave**  behave brave concave crave engrave forgave gave grave
knave pave rave save shave slave waive wave

**Cavern**  tavern (see *burn*)

**Caviar**  are bar bazaar bizarre car cigar czar disbar far guitar
jar par scar spar star tar

**Cavity**  depravity gravity

**Celebrate**  (see **Ate**)

**Cell**  bell belle caramel Carmel carrousel clientele dell dwell
excel farewell fell gel hell hotel infidel knell mademoiselle
personnel sell shell smell spell swell tell well yell

**Cellar**  dweller feller fortuneteller interstellar propeller
Rockefeller seller smeller speller stellar sweller teller

**Cello**  bellow fellow hello mellow Othello yellow

**Censor**  censer condenser denser dispenser fencer Spencer

**Cent**  (see **Bent**)

**Center**  dissenter enter experimenter frequenter inventor
    mentor presenter preventer renter tormentor

**C**

**Chain**  abstain again airplane arraign ascertain attain brain Cain
    campaign cane champagne cocaine complain contain crane
    detain disdain domain drain entertain explain feign gain
    grain humane hurricane hydroplane insane lane main
    Maine maintain mane migraine obtain ordain pain pane
    pertain plain plane profane propane rain refrain reign rein
    remain sane slain Spain sprain stain strain sustain train
    vain vane vein wane windowpane

**Chair**  (see **Air**)

**Champ**  amp camp clamp cramp damp lamp ramp stamp vamp

**Champagne**  (see **Chain**)

**Chance**  advance ants circumstance dance enhance
    extravagance finance France glance lance pants prance
    romance stance trance

**Change**  arrange derange estrange exchange range strange

**Channel**  flannel panel

**Chapel**  apple dapple grapple scrapple

**Charade**  (see **Afraid**)

**Charge**  barge discharge enlarge large

**Charm**  arm alarm disarm farm forearm harm

**Chaste**  baste aftertaste braced distaste faced freckle-faced
    haste hatchet-faced lambaste paste taste waist waste

**Chat**  (see **At**)

**Chauffeur**  gopher loafer (see *her*)

**Cheap**  barkeep cheep creep deep heap keep leap peep reap
    seep sheep sleep steep sweep weep

**Cheat**  athlete beat beet bittersweet bleat compete complete
    conceit concrete deceit defeat delete deplete discreet
    discrete eat elite feat feet fleet greet heat incomplete

indiscreet meat meet mistreat neat obsolete parakeet
receipt repeat retreat seat sheet sleet street suite sweet
treat wheat

**Cheated**  bleated competed completed conceited defeated
deleted depleted excreted greeted heated maltreated
pleated repeated retreated seated secreted
sleeted treated

**Check**  Czech deck fleck heck neck peck Quebec speck
trek wreck

**Cheer**  adhere appear atmosphere auctioneer beer
bombardier career cashier cavalier chandelier clear
dear deer disappear ear engineer fear financier frontier
gear hear hemisphere here insincere interfere jeer
lavaliere leer mere mountaineer near overhear overseer
peer persevere pioneer queer racketeer reappear rear
revere seer severe shear sheer sincere smear sneer spear
sphere stratosphere tear veneer volunteer year

**Cheese**  (see **Ease**)

**Chef**  clef deaf

**Cherry**  adversary airy arbitrary beneficiary berry bury
canary capillary cautionary commentary culinary
customary dairy dictionary dietary dignitary disciplinary
discretionary evolutionary extraordinary fairy February
ferry functionary hairy hereditary honorary imaginary
incendiary intermediary January Jerry legendary legionary
literary luminary Mary mercenary military momentary
monetary mortuary nary necessary obituary ordinary
Perry planetary prairie proprietary pulmonary reactionary
revolutionary sanctuary sanitary scary secretary seminary
sherry solitary stationary temporary Terry Tipperary very
visionary vocabulary voluntary wary

**C**

**Chess**  (see **Confess**)

**Chest**  arrest attest best blessed breast Bucharest Budapest
celeste congest contest crest detest digest divest dressed
guessed guest infest ingest interest invest jest manifest
messed nest pest protest request rest second-best
suggest test unrest vest zest

**Chew**  (see **Knew**)

**Chick**  (see **Brick**)

**Chicken**  quicken sicken stricken thicken (see in)

**Chief**  beef belief brief disbelief grief leaf relief thief

**Child**  dialed mild piled smiled wild

**Chill**  bill daffodil distill drill frill fulfill gill grill hill ill imbecile
instill kill mill nil quill shrill sill skill spill still swill thrill till
trill until whippoorwill will windmill windowsill

**Chilling**  (see **Willing**)

**Chime**  climb crime dime I'm lime mime pantomime prime
rhyme slime summertime thyme time

**Chin**  (see **Been**)

**Chip**  (see **Trip**)

**Chirp**  blurp burp chirp twirp usurp Wyatt Earp

**Chivalry**  delivery livery shivery slivery

**Choice**  invoice rejoice voice

**Choir**  (see **Fire**)

**Choke**  artichoke baroque bloke broke cloak coke croak
evoke folk invoke joke oak poke provoke revoke smoke
soak spoke stroke toke woke yoke

**Choose**  blues booze bruise cruise lose news ooze
snooze whose

**Chop**  (see **Drop**)

**Chopper**  (see **Proper**)

**Chore**  (see **Door**)

**Chorus** Brontosaurus sonorous Taurus thesaurus (see *us*)

**Chose** arose close compose decompose depose disclose dispose doze enclose expose foreclose froze goes hose impose indispose interpose knows nose owes pose predispose presuppose prose recompose rose suppose those toes transpose woes

**C**

**Christ** diced feist heist iced zeitgeist

**Christen** glisten listen

**Christianity** (see **Be**)

**Christmas** isthmus (see *us*)

**Chrome** chromosome comb dome foam gnome home honeycomb metronome Nome poem roam Rome tome

**Chuckle** arbuckle buckle honeysuckle knuckle suckle

**Chunk** bunk chunk cyberpunk drunk dunk flunk funk hunk junk monk plunk punk shrunk skunk slunk spunk stunk sunk trunk

**Church** besmirch birch lurch perch research search smirch

**Cigar** are bar bazaar bizarre car caviar czar disbar far guitar jar par scar spar star tar

**Cinch** flinch inch lynch pinch

**Cinematic** (see **Attic**)

**Citizen** amen den fen hen hydrogen Ken men oxygen pen regimen specimen ten then yen zen

**City** committee ditty gritty kitty pity pretty self-pity witty

**Civil** drivel shrivel snivel swivel

**Class** alas amass ass bass brass crass gas glass grass harass hourglass lass looking-glass mass morass mustache overpass pass sass sassafras surpass

**Claw** Arkansas awe bra caw claw draw flaw gnaw guffaw hurrah jaw law Ma macaw nah overdraw Pa paw raw saw seesaw shah slaw squaw straw thaw withdraw

**C**

**Clean** bean between caffeine canteen chlorine codeine Colleen convene cuisine dean demean evergreen Florentine foreseen gasoline Gene green guillotine Halloween in-between intervene kerosene lean lien machine marine mean mezzanine Nazarene nectarine nicotine obscene preen quarantine queen ravine routine sardine scene seen serene spleen submarine tambourine tangerine teen thirteen (etc.) Vaseline velveteen wintergreen wolverine

**Cleanse** bends dens lens mends sends tends

**Clearance** adherence appearance coherence disappearance incoherence interference perseverance

**Clerk** handiwork irk jerk Kirk lurk murk overwork perk quirk shirk smirk Turk work

**Clever** endeavor ever forever however lever never sever whatever whenever wherever whoever

**Client** compliant defiant giant reliant self-reliant

**Cliff** handkerchief if sniff stiff tiff whiff

**Climate** primate (see *it, ate*)

**Climatic** (see **Attic**)

**Climb** chime crime dime I'm lime mime pantomime prime rhyme slime summertime thyme time

**Clock** Bangkok beanstalk boondock cock cornstalk crock deadlock defrock dock flintlock flock frock gawk gridlock hawk hock J. S. Bach jock knock Little Rock livestock lock mock Mohawk padlock peacock rock shock sidewalk small talk smock sock squawk stalk stock talk tomahawk unlock walk wok

**Clog** analog bog catalog cog fog demagogue dialogue dog epilogue flog frog grog hog jog log monologue synagogue travelogue

**Close**　adios bellicose comatose diagnose dose engross
　　　grandiose gross morose nose overdose varicose verbose

**Close**　arose chose compose decompose depose disclose
　　　dispose doze enclose expose foreclose froze goes hose
　　　impose indispose interpose knows nose owes pose
　　　predispose presuppose prose recompose rose suppose
　　　those toes transpose woes

**Cloth**　broth froth moth swath wroth

**Cloud**　allowed aloud crowd enshroud loud plowed proud
　　　shroud thundercloud

**Cloudy**　cum laude dowdy howdy rowdy

**Clover**　Dover drover moreover over rover (see *her*)

**Clown**　brown crown down downtown drown frown gown
　　　hand-me-down noun renown town tumble-down upside
　　　down uptown

**Club**　Beelzebub bub cub grub hub hubbub pub rub rub-a-dub-
　　　dub scrub shrub snub stub sub tub

**Clue**　(see **Do**)

**Clutch**　crutch Dutch hutch inasmuch much retouch
　　　such touch

**Coach**　approach broach cockroach encroach poach
　　　reproach roach

**Coal**　(see **Control**)

**Coarse**　course divorce endorse force horse Norse reinforce
　　　remorse resource source

**Coast**　boast foremost furthermost ghost host innermost
　　　most post roast toast whipping post

**Coastal**　postal

**Coat**　(see **Boat**)

**Coax**　cholks folks hoax jokes polks smokes spokes yokes

**Cockroach**　approach broach coach encroach poach
　　　reproach roach

61

**Code** (see **Road**)

**Coffee** toffee (see *me*)

**Coffin** coughin' often soften

**C**

**Coherent** adherent incoherent inherent perseverant

**Coil** broil foil loyal oil recoil royal spoil toil turmoil

**Coin** Des Moines groin join loin purloin sirloin tenderloin

**Coincidence** (see **Fence**)

**Cold** behold blindfold bold centerfold fold foothold foretold
gold hold household marigold mold old retold scold sold
told uphold withhold

**Collapse** caps craps elapse flaps lapse maps naps perhaps
saps traps wraps

**Collar** bawler brawler call 'er caller choler crawler dollar
hauler mauler scrawler smaller squalor taller

**Collect** (see **Defect**)

**Collection** (see **Affection**)

**College** acknowledge knowledge (see *ledge*)

**Collision** (see **Vision**)

**Color** discolor duller sculler Technicolor

**Coma** aroma diploma sarcoma Sonoma Tacoma

**Comb** chrome chromosome dome foam gnome home
honeycomb metronome Nome poem roam Rome tome

**Come** album aquarium auditorium become bum burdensome
Christendom cranium crematorium crumb curriculum
drum dumb emporium fee-fi-fo-fum glum gum gymnasium
hum kettledrum kingdom martyrdom maximum
meddlesome medium millennium minimum mum museum
numb opium overcome pendulum petroleum platinum
plum premium quarrelsome radium random rum
sanitarium scum slum some strum succumb sum swum
tedium thumb Tom Thumb Tweedledum uranium
worrisome yum

**Comedy**  (see **Be**)

**Comfort**  (see **Court**)

**Comic**  atomic anatomic economic

**Commercial**  controversial

**Commune**  attune dune immune impugn inopportune June
    tune (see *moon*)

**Communicate**  (see **Ate**)

**Company**  (see **Be**)

**Complain**  (see **Chain**)

**Complete**  athlete beat beet bittersweet bleat cheat
    complete conceit concrete deceit defeat delete deplete
    discreet discrete eat elite feat feet fleet greet heat
    incomplete indiscreet meat meet mistreat neat obsolete
    parakeet receipt repeat retreat seat sheet sleet street
    suite sweet treat wheat

**Complex**  decks duplex ex flex necks pecks reflex Rolidex
    specs Tex unisex

**Complexion**  (see **Affection**)

**Complicate**  (see **Ate**)

**Compliment**  (see **Cent**)

**Compute**  (see **Cute**)

**Computer**  (see **Suitor**)

**Con**  Amazon autobahn Babylon bonbon Bonn brawn chiffon
    dawn drawn echelon fawn gone lawn neon on pawn
    pentagon silicon swan undergone upon wan woebegone
    wonton yawn

**Concentrate**  (see **Ate**)

**Concern**  adjourn burn churn discern earn fern intern kern
    learn overturn return sojourn spurn stern taciturn turn
    urn yearn

**C**

**Concert** (see **Hurt**)

**Concrete** (see **Sweet**)

**Condemn** Bethlehem gem hem phlegm requiem stem them

**Condition** acquisition addition admission ambition
ammunition attrition audition coalition commission
competition composition definition demolition deposition
disposition edition electrician emission exhibition
expedition exposition extradition fission ignition
imposition inhibition inquisition intermission intuition
magician mathematician mission musician nutrition
omission opposition partition permission petition
physician politician position prohibition proposition
recognition rendition repetition requisition statistician
submission superstition technician tradition transmission
transposition transition tuition (see *in*)

**Conduct** abduct construct deduct instruct obstruct
plucked viaduct

**Confess** access address baroness bashfulness bitterness
bless caress chess cleverness cloudiness compress
craziness deadliness depress digress distress dizziness
dress duress eagerness easiness eeriness emptiness
excess express finesse foolishness ghostliness guess
happiness haziness homelessness idleness impress
joyfulness joylessness laziness less limitless Loch Ness
lustfulness mess nervousness obsess openness oppress
outrageousness penniless playfulness possess press
profess progress queasiness recess regress repossess
repress rockiness seediness shallowness silkiness
sleaziness sleepiness sneakiness SOS spaciousness
spitefulness stress success suppress thoughtfulness
transgress uselessness viciousness willingness wishfulness
worldliness yes youthfulness

**Confession**  aggression compression concession depression
digression discretion expression impression indiscretion
obsession oppression possession procession profession
progression recession regression repression secession
session succession suppression transgression

**Confetti**  jetty machete petty spaghetti sweaty

**Confidential**  credential deferential differential essential
existential influential nonessential potential preferential
presidential providential prudential quintessential
residential sequential torrential

**Conflict**  addict constrict contradict convict derelict evict
flicked inflict licked predict pricked strict

**Conform**  chloroform conform deform form inform norm
perform rainstorm reform snowstorm storm swarm
transform uniform warm

**Confuse**  abuse accuse cues deduce diffuse disuse duce
excuse induce infuse introduce juice misuse obtuse
peruse produce profuse reduce refuse reproduce seduce
Syracuse use

**Conquer**  conker honker

**Consist**  (see **Exist**)

**Contain**  (see **Chain**)

**Contribution**  (see *revolution*)

**Control**  bowl buttonhole cajole casserole coal dole droll
enroll goal hole loophole Maypole mole Old King Cole
oriole parole patrol pole poll porthole role roll scroll
tadpole toll troll whole

**Convention**  (see **Tension**)

**Converge**  (see **Verge**)

**Convince**  hints mints prince rinse since wince

**Cook**  book brook crook hook look mistook nook outlook
rook shook took undertook

**C**

**Cool** April fool drool fool ghoul Liverpool overrule pool rule
school spool stool tool whirlpool

**Cop** chop crop drop eavesdrop flop hop lollipop mop plop
pop prop raindrop shop stop swap tip-top whop

**Cope** antelope cantaloupe dope elope envelope grope
gyroscope hope horoscope kaleidoscope microscope
mope pope rope scope slope soap stethoscope telescope

**Core** (see **Door**)

**Cork** fork New York pork torque stork uncork

**Corn** adorn airborne born Cape Horn Capricorn horn
lovelorn Matterhorn morn mourn popcorn scorn
stillborn sworn unicorn warn worn

**Corny** horny thorny

**Correct** (see **Defect**)

**Corrupt** abrupt cupped disrupt erupt interrupt supped

**Cost** bossed crossed exhaust flossed frost holocaust lost
Pentecost tossed

**Cottage** wattage

**Cotton** begotten gotten forgotten rotten

**Couch** crouch grouch ouch pouch slouch vouch

**Cough** off scoff trough

**Could** brotherhood fatherhood firewood good Hollywood
hood likelihood livelihood misunderstood motherhood
neighborhood should sisterhood stood understood
withstood womanhood wood would

**Count** account amount dismount fount mount
paramount tantamount

**Couple** supple

**Course** coarse divorce endorse force horse Norse reinforce
remorse resource source

**Court** abort assort cavort comfort contort davenport deport
distort escort exhort export extort fort import passport

port quart report resort retort short snort sort sport
support thwart tort transport wart

**Cousin**  buzzin' cussin' dozen fusin' musin'

**Cove**  by Jove clove dove drove grove rove

**Cover**  discover hover lover recover rediscover shover
undercover (see *her*)

**Cow**  allow avow bough bow brow chow disavow endow frau
how kowtow now ow plough plow row slough somehow
sow thou vow wow

**Coy**  (see **Boy**)

**Crab**  blab cab dab drab gab grab jab lab nab scab slab stab tab

**Crabby**  abbey cabby flabby grabby scabby shabby tabby

**Craft**  draft draught graft overdraft witchcraft

**Cranky**  bank blank clank crank dank drank flank frank hank
outrank plank prank rank sank shrank spank stank tank
thank yank

**Cranky**  hanky lanky Yankee

**Craze**  ablaze amaze appraise bays braze days daze faze gaze
glaze graze haze malaise mayonnaise maze nays nowadays
plays polonaise praise ways

**Crazy**  daisy hazy lazy

**Cream**  beam deem dream esteem extreme gleam ream
regime scheme scream seam seen steam stream supreme
team teem

**Creative**  (see **Native**)

**Creature**  bleacher feature preacher screecher teacher

**Credit**  accredit discredit edit (see *it*)

**Crept**  accept adept except intercept kept overslept slept
stepped swept wept

**Crew**  (see **Do**)

**Cricket**  picket thicket ticket wicket (see *it*)

**C**

**Crime** chime climb dime I'm lime mime pantomime prime
rhyme slime summertime thyme time

**Cringe** binge fringe hinge infringe singe

**Crisp** lisp wisp

**Critic** analytic arthritic hypocritic paralytic parasitic
Semitic (see *tick*)

**Critical** analytical political

**Crock** (see **Clock**)

**Crocodile** (see **Smile**)

**Cross** across albatross boss double-cross floss gloss loss moss
rhinoceros sauce toss

**Crow** afro although banjo beau below bestow blow bow
buffalo bungalow calico crossbow depot doe domino
dough embryo escrow Eskimo flow foe forgo fro gazebo
gigolo glow go grow heigh-ho ho-ho hobo hoe incognito
indigo Joe know long ago low Mexico mistletoe mow no
oboe oh outgrow overflow overgrow overthrow owe
Pinocchio pistachio plateau quo rainbow ratio roe row
sew slow snow so Soho status quo stow studio tally-ho
though throw tiptoe to-and-fro toe Tokyo tow tremolo
undergo undertow vertigo woe yo yo-yo

**Crowd** allowed aloud cloud enshroud loud plowed proud
shroud thundercloud

**Crown** (see **Clown**)

**Crucifix** acrobatics bics fiddlesticks fix kicks licks
mathematics mix nix picks politics six sticks Styx ticks
transfix tricks wicks

**Crucifixion** addiction affliction benediction contradiction
conviction depiction diction eviction fiction friction
jurisdiction prediction restriction

**C**

**Crude**  brood clued conclude dude exclude food glued
include intrude misconstrued mood preclude prude
rude seclude shrewd wooed

**Cruel**  duel fuel jewel

**Crumb**  (see **Dumb**)

**Crumble**  bumble fumble grumble humble jumble mumble
rumble stumble tumble

**Crusade**  (see **Afraid**)

**Crush**  blush brush flush gush lush mush plush rush slush
thrush underbrush

**Crutch**  clutch Dutch hutch inasmuch much retouch
such touch

**Cry**  alibi amplify banzai barfly butterfly buy by bye certify
clarify crucify defy deify deny die dignify diversify
dragonfly drive-by dry dye eye firefly fly fry glorify gratify
guy high horrify I identify imply July justify lie lullaby
modify my mystify notify passerby pie pry qualify rely
rye satisfy sci-fi shy sigh signify simplify sky sly specify spry
spy terrify testify thigh tie try underlie verify why

**Crypt**  chipped dipped equipped manuscript script sipped
transcript whipped zipped

**Crystal**  pistol

**Cuba**  scuba tuba

**Cube**  boob rube tube

**Cucumber**  cumber encumber lumber number
slumber umber

**Cuddle**  fuddle huddle muddle puddle

**Cue**  (see **Knew**)

**Cuff**  (see **Bluff**)

**Culture**  agriculture vulture

**Cup**  buttercup fed up hard-up pick-up pup sup up

**C**

**Cupid** stupid

**Curb** blurb 'burb disturb herb perturb Serb suburb
superb verb

**Cure** allure armature assure brochure caricature cocksure
demure endure ensure expenditure forfeiture immature
impure insecure insure liqueur literature lure manicure
mature miniature obscure overture pedicure premature
pure reassure secure signature sure tablature
temperature your

**Curious** (see **Us**)

**Curl** earl girl hurl pearl swirl twirl whirl

**Curly** burly curly girlie pearly squirrelly surly swirly

**Curse** adverse converse disburse disperse diverse hearse
immerse intersperse inverse nurse purse rehearse
reverse terse transverse traverse universe verse worse

**Curt** (see **Hurt**)

**Curve** conserve deserve nerve observe preserve reserve
serve swerve

**Cuss** (see **Us**)

**Custody** (see **Be**)

**Cut** but butt glut gut halibut hut King Tut mutt nut putt rut
scuttlebutt shut smut strut uncut

**Cute** absolute acute astute attribute beaut boot brute Butte
chute commute compute constitute coot destitute
dilute dispute disrepute dissolute electrocute enroute
execute flute fruit hoot loot lute minute moot mute
newt parachute persecute pollute prosecute prostitute
pursuit recruit refute repute resolute root route scoot
shoot snoot substitute suit toot transmute uproot

# D

**Dad**  (see **Mad**)

**Daddy**  baddy caddie laddie paddy sugar daddy

**Dagger**  carpetbagger stagger swagger

**Daily**  Bailey gaily Israeli ukulele

**Dairy**  (see **Cherry**)

**Daisy**  crazy hazy lazy

**Damn**  (see **Am**)

**Dance**  advance ants chance circumstance enhance
extravagance finance France glance lance pants prance
romance stance trance

**Dandelion**  buyin' cryin' denyin' dyin' lion lyin' Orion Ryan
sighin' tryin' Zion (see *in*)

**Dang**  bang boomerang clang fang orangutan rang sang
slang sprang

**Dangerous**  (see **Us**)

**Dare**  (see **Air**)

**Dark**  aardvark arc ark bark embark hark lark mark narc park
patriarch remark shark spark stark

**Dart**  apart art cart chart counterpart depart heart mart part
smart start sweetheart tart upstart

**Dash**  ash balderdash bash brash cash clash crash flash gnash
rash rehash slash smash splash stash thrash trash

**Date**  (see **Ate**)

**Daughter**  blotter hotter otter plotter slaughter spotter
squatter trotter water

**Dawn**  Amazon Babylon begone bonbon Bonn brawn chiffon
con Don drawn fawn gone hexagon John lawn lexicon
octagon on Oregon pawn pentagon silicon undergone
upon withdrawn wanton yawn

**D**

**Day** array bay betray bluejay bouquet bray clay decay delay
disarray dismay display eh? essay exposé fray gay gray
hay hey holiday hooray José Kay lay matinee may moiré
naysay negligée obey pay play portray protégé ray résumé
ricochet risqué rosé say slay sleigh soufflé stay stray sway
they toupee way weigh x-ray

**Dead** ahead bed bedspread bread bred coed dread fed
figurehead fled flowerbed fountainhead gingerbread head
inbred lead led misled misread overfed read red riverbed
said shed shred sled sped spread thoroughbred thread
underfed unthread wed

**Deaf** chef clef

**Deal** (see **Feel**)

**Dealer** congealer feeler healer reeler sealer squealer
stealer wheeler

**Dear** (see **Near**)

**Death** breath Macbeth

**Debate** (see **Ate**)

**Debt** alphabet bayonet bet brunette cabinet cadet cigarette
clarinet cornet corvette duet epithet etiquette forget
fret gazette get jet Joliet Juliet let luncheonette
marionette met net omelet pet quartet regret roulette
set silhouette Somerset sunset sweat threat Tibet toilette
upset vet 'vette violet wet yet

**Decay** (see **Say**)

**Decease** cease crease decrease fleece geese grease Greece
increase lease mantelpiece masterpiece peace piece
police release

**Decent** indecent recent

**Deception** conception contraception exception inception
perception preconception reception self-deception

**Decision** (see **Vision**)

**Deck** check Czech fleck heck neck peck Quebec speck
　　trek wreck

**Decline** (see **Fine**)

**Decoy** (see **Boy**)

**Dedicate** (see **Ate**)

**Deduct** abduct conduct construct instruct obstruct
　　plucked viaduct

**Deep** barkeep cheep creep heap keep leap peep reap seep
　　sheep sleep steep sweep weep

**Defeat** athlete beat beet bittersweet bleat cheat compete
　　complete conceit concrete deceit delete deplete discreet
　　discrete eat elite feat feet fleet greet heat incomplete
　　indiscreet meat meet mistreat neat obsolete parakeet
　　receipt repeat retreat seat sheet sleet street suite sweet
　　treat wheat

**Defect** affect architect bisect checked collect connect correct
　　deflect dialect direct disinfect dissect effect eject erect
　　expect genuflect incorrect inject neglect object pecked
　　perfect project prospect protect recollect reflect reject
　　respect select subject suspect wrecked

**Defendant** ascendant attendant dependent descendant
　　independent pendant superintendent transcendent

**Defender** (see **Tender**)

**Defense** (see **Fence**)

**Defensive** apprehensive comprehensive expensive extensive
　　incomprehensive inexpensive intensive offensive pensive

**Defer** amateur blur chauffeur concur confer connoisseur
　　demur deter fur her incur infer Jennifer myrrh occur
　　per prefer purr recur sir slur spur stir transfer voyageur
　　were whir

**Defiance** alliance appliance compliance reliance

**D**

**Degree** (see **Be**)

**Delay** (see **Say**)

**Deli**  belly jelly Kelly Shelly smelly

**Delicious** (see **Vicious**)

**Delight** (see **Flight**)

**Deliver**  giver liver quiver river shiver sliver (see *her*)

**Delivery**  chivalry livery shivery slivery quivery

**Demand**  and band brand canned command contraband
   expand fanned grand hand land panned planned
   reprimand Rio Grande sand stand

**Demo**  memo

**Demolish**  (See **Abolish**)

**Denial**  dial retrial self-denial trial viol (see *vile*)

**Dent** (see **Bent**)

**Dental** (see **Gentle**)

**Dentist**  apprenticed

**Deny** (see **Cry**)

**Depart**  apart art cart chart counterpart dart heart mart part
   smart start sweetheart tart upstart

**Depot** (see **Blow**)

**Depression**  aggression compression concession confession
   digression discretion expression impression indiscretion
   obsession oppression possession procession profession
   progression recession regression repression secession
   session succession suppression transgression

**Deputy** (see **Be**)

**Describe**  bribe circumscribe jibe prescribe scribe
   subscribe tribe

**Deserve**  conserve curve nerve observe preserve reserve
   serve swerve

**Desire**  acquire admire amplifier aspire attire buyer choir
   conspire crier cryer dire drier dryer entire esquire expire

fire flier friar higher hire inquire inspire justifier liar
magnifier multiplier mystifier perspire prior prophesier
require retire satisfier sire squire supplier testifier tire
transpire wire

**D**

**Desk**  burlesque grotesque picturesque

**Desperado**  bravado Colorado El Dorado Laredo
Mikado tornado

**Dessert**  alert avert blurt concert convert curt desert dirt
divert exert expert extrovert flirt hurt insert introvert
invert pervert shirt skirt squirt subvert yogurt

**Destroy**  (see **Boy**)

**Deviate**  abbreviate alleviate (see *ate*)

**Devil**  bedevil bevel dishevel level revel

**Diagnosis**  narcosis neurosis prognosis psychosis

**Dial**  denial retrial self-denial trial viol (see *vile*)

**Diary**  fiery priory Valkyrie wiry

**Dice**  advice concise device entice ice lice mice nice paradise
precise price rice sacrifice spice splice suffice thrice
twice vice

**Dictate**  (see **Ate**)

**Did**  bid forbid grid hid invalid lid Madrid pyramid rid skid
slid squid

**Die**  (see **Cry**)

**Died**  beside bonafide bride collide confide countryside decide
defied died dignified divide eyed fireside guide hide hillside
homicide inside lied outside override pride provide reside
ride side slide snide stride subdivide subside suicide tide
tried wide yuletide

**Diet**  riot quiet (see *it*)

**Differ**  sniffer stiffer (see *her*)

**Difference**  (see **Fence**)

**Dig**  big dig fig gig jig pig renege rig swig twig wig

75

**Digest** (see **Best**)

**Digit** fidget midget widget

**Dignify** signify (see *cry*)

**Dime** chime climb crime I'm lime mime pantomime prime
rhyme slime summertime thyme time

**D**

**Dimension** (see **Tension**)

**Dimple** pimple simple

**Dine** (see **Fine**)

**Diner** cosigner designer eyeliner finer liner miner minor
refiner shiner signer

**Dinner** B. F. Skinner beginner breadwinner inner sinner
skinner spinner thinner

**Dinosaur** (see **Door**)

**Dip** (see **Trip**)

**Diploma** aroma coma sarcoma Sonoma Tacoma

**Direct** (see **Defect**)

**Direction** (see **Affection**)

**Director** collector connector detector deflector injector
inspector nectar objector projector prospector protector
reflector selector vector (see *her*)

**Directory** rectory

**Dirt** (see **Hurt**)

**Dirty** flirty thirty

**Disco** Cisco Crisco San Francisco

**Discuss** (see **Us**)

**Disease** aborigines appease bees breeze cheese ease
expertise freeze Hercules keys knees peas pleas please
sees seize Siamese sleaze squeeze tease trapeze 'zzzs

**Disgrace** ace base bass brace case chase commonplace
debase displace embrace encase erase face grace lace
mace misplace pace place race replace space steeplechase
trace unlace vase

**Disgust**  adjust August bust crust distrust encrust entrust gust just lust mistrust must robust rust thrust trust unjust

**Dish**  devilish fish gibberish impoverish squish swish wish

**Dismay**  (see **Say**)

**D**

**Distance**  assistance consistence existence insistence persistence resistance subsistence

**Distant**  assistant consistent existent inconsistent insistent persistent resistant subsistent

**Distaste**  baste aftertaste braced chaste faced freckle-faced haste hatchet-faced paste taste waist waste

**Distinction**  extinction

**Distort**  (see **Court**)

**Distortion**  abortion contortion extortion portion proportion

**Ditch**  bewitch bitch ditch enrich glitch hitch pitch rich snitch stitch switch twitch which

**Divinity**  (see **Be**)

**Divorce**  coarse course endorse force horse Norse reinforce remorse resource source

**Dizzy**  busy frizzy Lizzie tin lizzie tizzy

**Do**  accrue ado bamboo blew blue boo boohoo brew caribou cashew clue construe coo coup crew cuckoo drew flew flue glue gnu goo grew Hindu hitherto hullabaloo igloo impromptu into issue Kalamazoo kangaroo kazoo kickapoo misconstrue moo outdo overdo overthrew peekaboo Peru poo rendezvous screw shampoo shoe shoo shrew Sioux slew slue stew taboo tattoo threw through tissue to too true two undo voodoo wahoo well-to-do who withdrew woo yahoo zoo Zulu (see *you*)

**Dock**  (see **Clock**)

**Dodge**  dislodge hodgepodge lodge

**Does**  abuzz buzz cause coz fuzz was

**D**

**Dog**  analog bog catalog clog cog fog demagogue dialogue epilogue flog frog grog hog jog log monologue synagogue travelogue underdog

**Dole**  (see **Control**)

**Dollar**  bawler brawler call 'er caller choler collar crawler hauler mauler scrawler smaller squalor taller

**Dolly**  collie finale folly golly jolly melancholy Molly Polly tamale trolley volley

**Donate**  (see **Ate**)

**Done**  anyone begun bun comparison everyone fun Galveston gun hon Hun jettison none nun oblivion one outdone outrun overdone overrun phenomenon pun run shun simpleton skeleton son stun sun ton unison venison won

**Doom**  bloom boom broom cloakroom entomb flume gloom groom room tomb whom womb zoom

**Door**  abhor ambassador ashore auditor bachelor Baltimore before boar bore chancellor chore commodore competitor conspirator contributor core corps corridor deplore dinosaur drawer Ecuador editor emperor encore evermore explore exterior floor folklore for fore four furthermore galore governor ignore implore inferior lore matador metaphor more nevermore nor oar offshore or orator ore poor pour rapport restore roar score seashore senator señor shore Singapore snore soar sophomore sore spore store swore therefore Thor tore troubadour underscore uproar visitor yore your

**Dope**  (see **Hope**)

**Dose**  adios bellicose close comatose diagnose engross grandiose gross morose nose overdose varicose verbose

**Double**  bubble rubble stubble trouble

**Doubt**  about boy scout blow-out bout clout devout eke out flout gout lout out pout roundabout route scout shout snout spout sprout stout tout trout wash-out worn-out

**Dove**  above glove ladylove love mourning dove of shove turtle dove

**Dove**  by Jove clove cove drove grove rove

**Down**  brown clown crown downtown drown frown gown hand-me-down noun renown town tumble-down upside down uptown

**Dozen**  buzzin' cousin cussin' fusin' musin'

**Draft**  craft draught graft overdraft witchcraft

**Drafted**  grafted shafted (see *did*)

**Drag**  bag brag flag gag hag lag mag nag rag sag shag slag snag stag swag tag wag

**Drama**  Bahama comma Dalai Lama llama mamma melodrama pajama Yokohama

**Drank**  bank blank clank crank dank flank frank hank outrank plank prank rank sank shrank spank stank tank thank yank

**Drastic**  bombastic elastic enthusiastic fantastic gymnastic iconoclastic plastic sarcastic scholastic spastic

**Draw**  Arkansas awe bra caw claw flaw gnaw guffaw hurrah jaw law Ma macaw nah overdraw Pa paw raw saw seesaw shah slaw squaw straw thaw withdraw

**Drawn**  (see **Dawn**)

**Dread**  (see **Said**)

**Dream**  beam cream deem esteem extreme gleam ream regime scheme scream seam seen steam stream supreme team teem

**Dreamt**  attempt contempt exempt tempt unkempt

**Dreamy**  creamy seamy steamy (see *me*)

**Dress**  (see **Confess**)

**D**

**Dressy** messy

**Drew** (see **Do**)

**Drift** gift lift shift spendthrift swift thrift

**Drill** (see **Fill**)

**Drink** blink brink chink clink fink hoodwink ink kink link mink
pink rink shrink sink slink stink wink zinc

**Drizzle** chisel fizzle frizzle grizzle sizzle swizzle

**Drop** chop cop crop eavesdrop flop hop lollipop mop plop
pop prop raindrop shop stop swap tip-top whop

**Drove** by Jove clove cove dove grove rove

**Drug** bug dug jug hug lug mug plug pug rug shrug slug smug
snug thug tug

**Drum** (see **Dumb**)

**Drummer** comer dumber hummer newcomer
strummer summer

**Drunk** bunk chunk clunk cyberpunk dunk flunk funk hunk
junk monk plunk punk shrunk skunk slunk spunk stunk
sunk trunk

**Drunken** shrunken sunken

**Dry** alibi amplify banzai barfly butterfly buy by bye certify
clarify crucify cry defy deify deny die dignify diversify
dragonfly drive-by dye eye firefly fly fry glorify gratify
guy high horrify I identify imply July justify lie lullaby
modify my mystify notify passerby pie pry qualify rely
rye satisfy sci-fi shy sigh signify simplify sky sly specify spry
spy terrify testify thigh tie try underlie verify why

**Duce** (see **Abuse**)

**Duck** (see **Truck**)

**Dude** (see **Feud, Mood**)

**Dudgeon** bludgeon

**Due** (see **Knew**)

**Duel**  cruel fuel jewel perusal renewal

**Dug**  bug drug jug hug lug mug plug pug rug shrug slug smug snug thug tug

**Duke**  juke puke uke

**Dull**  annul cull gull hull lull mull scull skull

**D**

**Dumb**  album aquarium auditorium become bum burdensome Christendom come cranium crematorium crumb curriculum drum emporium fee-fi-fo-fum glum gum gymnasium hum kettledrum kingdom martyrdom maximum meddlesome medium millennium minimum mum museum numb opium overcome pendulum petroleum platinum plum premium quarrelsome radium random rum sanitarium scum slum some strum succumb sum swum tedium thumb Tom Thumb Tweedledum uranium worrisome yum

**Dummy**  crummy gummy mummy rummy tummy yummy

**Dump**  bump chump clump hump jump lump plump rump slump stump thump trump ump

**Dupe**  coop droop group hoop loop nincompoop poop scoop sloop soup stoop swoop troop troupe whoop

**Duplex**  complex decks ex flex necks pecks reflex Rolidex sex specs Tex unisex

**During**  alluring assuring blurring concurring conferring curing deferring demurring deterring enduring ensuring incurring inferring insuring interring luring maturing occurring preferring procuring purring referring securing spurring transferring whirring

**Dusk**  husk musk tusk

**Duty**  beauty cutie

**Dwarf**  wharf

**Dwindle**  kindle rekindle spindle swindle

**Dynamic**  ceramic Islamic panoramic

# E

**Each**  beach breach impeach leech peach preach reach screech
speech teach

**Eager**  beleaguer intriguer leaguer meager overeager

**Eagle**  beagle illegal legal regal sea gull

**Ear**  adhere appear atmosphere auctioneer beer bombardier
career cashier cavalier chandelier cheer clear dear deer
disappear engineer fear financier frontier gear hear
hemisphere here insincere interfere jeer lavaliere leer
mere mountaineer near overhear overseer peer
persevere pioneer queer racketeer reappear rear revere
seer severe shear sheer sincere smear sneer spear sphere
stratosphere tear veneer volunteer year

**Earn**  adjourn burn churn concern discern fern intern
kern learn overturn return sojourn spurn stern taciturn
turn urn yearn

**Earth**  birth dearth girth mirth worth

**Ease**  aborigines appease bees breeze cheese disease expertise
freeze Hercules keys knees peas pleas please sees seize
Siamese sleaze squeeze tease trapeze 'zzzs

**Easel**  diesel measle weasel

**East**  beast ceased creased deceased feast least pieced
priest yeast

**Easy**  breezy cheesy greasy queasy sleazy sneezy
speakeasy wheezy

**Eat**  athlete beat beet bittersweet bleat cheat compete
complete conceit concrete deceit defeat delete deplete
discreet discrete elite feat feet fleet greet heat incomplete

indiscreet meat meet mistreat neat obsolete parakeet receipt repeat retreat seat sheet sleet street suite sweet treat wheat

**Ebb**  deb web

**Ebony**  (see **Be**)

**Echo**  art deco deco gecko (see *glow*)

**Ecstasy**  (see **Be**)

**Eden**  leadin' needin' readin' seedin' Sweden weedin'

**Edge**  allege dredge fledge hedge ledge privilege sacrilege sledge wedge

**Educate**  (see **Ate**)

**Effect**  affect architect bisect checked collect connect correct defect deflect dialect direct disinfect dissect eject erect expect genuflect incorrect inject neglect object pecked perfect project prospect protect recollect reflect reject respect select subject suspect wrecked

**Either**  breather neither

**Elapse**  caps collapse craps flaps lapse maps naps perhaps saps traps wraps

**Election**  (see **Affection**)

**Elf**  herself himself itself myself self shelf yourself

**Elm**  helm realm overwhelm whelm

**Elope**  (see **Hope**)

**Embargo**  argot cargo Fargo largo

**Embrace**  ace  base bass brace case chase commonplace debase disgrace displace encase erase face grace lace mace misplace pace place race replace space steeplechase trace unlace vase

**Emerge**  (see **Verge**)

**E**

**E**

**Emotion** commotion locomotion lotion motion notion ocean potion promotion

**Emperor** (see **Door**)

**Enchant** (see **Ant**)

**Encore** (see **Door**)

**End** apprehend ascend attend befriend bend blend commend comprehend condescend defend depend descend dividend expend extend fend friend intend lend mend offend penned pretend recommend send spend suspend tend transcend trend unbend

**Ended** amended apprehended ascended attended befriended bended blended commended comprehended condescended contended defended depended descended expended extended fended intended mended misapprehended offended portended pretended recommended splendid suspended tended unattended unblended

**Endurance** assurance insurance

**Endure** (see **Cure**)

**Enemy** (see **Be**)

**Energy** (see **Be**)

**Enjoy** ahoy annoy boy buoy convoy corduroy coy decoy destroy employ Illinois joy ploy Roy Savoy soy toy troy viceroy

**Enough** bluff buff cuff duff fluff gruff huff muff powder puff rough scruff scuff snuff stuff tough

**Enter** center dissenter experimenter frequenter inventor mentor presenter preventer renter tormenter

**Entry** gentry sentry

**Envelope** (see **Hope**)

**Episode**  (see **Road**)

**Equal**  sequel

**Equation**  abrasion dissuasion evasion invasion
occasion persuasion

**Erase**  (see **Embrace**)

**Erect**  (see **Effect**)

**E**

**Erotic**  chaotic exotic hypnotic idiotic macrobiotic narcotic
neurotic quixotic

**Erratic**  (see **Attic**)

**Error**  bearer carer darer terror wearer

**Erupt**  abrupt corrupt cupped disrupt interrupt supped

**Escape**  ape cape cityscape drape grape landscape seascape
shape tape

**Essence**  adolescence convalescence fluorescence
incandescence obsolescence

**Esteem**  beam cream deem dream extreme gleam ream
regime scheme scream seam seen steam stream supreme
team teem

**Eternal**  colonel external fraternal infernal internal journal
kernel maternal nocturnal paternal

**Eternity**  fraternity maternity paternity

**European**  Caribbean Crimean Galilean peon (see *in*)

**Evangelist**  (see **Exist**)

**Evasive**  dissuasive invasive persuasive pervasive

**Eve**  achieve believe bereave conceive disbelieve grieve
heave leave perceive receive relieve reprieve retrieve
sleeve weave

**Evening**  (see **Sing**)

**Event**  (see **Bent**)

**Eventful**  resentful

**Everyone**  anyone begun bun comparison done fun Galveston
gun hon Hun jettison none nun oblivion one outdone
outrun overdone overrun phenomenon pun run shun
simpleton skeleton son stun sun ton unison venison won

**Everything**  (see **Sing**)

**E**

**Evict**  addict conflict constrict contradict convict derelict
flicked inflict licked predict pricked strict

**Evil**  medieval primeval upheaval weevil

**Evolution**  (see **Revolution**)

**Ex**  complex decks duplex flex necks pecks reflex Rolidex sex
specs Tex unisex

**Exact**  (see **Act**)

**Examine**  famine

**Example**  ample sample trample

**Except**  accept adept crept intercept kept overslept slept
stepped swept wept

**Exception**  conception contraception deception inception
perception preconception reception self-deception

**Excite**  appetite bite blight bright byte contrite copyright
daylight delight despite dynamite Fahrenheit fight flight
fright headlight height ignite invite kite knight light
midnight might moonlight night outright parasite plight
polite quite recite reunite right satellite sight site sleight
slight spite starlight sunlight tight trite twilight unite
white write

**Excuse**  abuse accuse confuse cues deduce diffuse disuse
duce induce infuse introduce juice misuse obtuse
peruse produce profuse reduce refuse reproduce seduce
Syracuse use

**Execution**  (see **Revolution**)

**Exhibit**  inhibit prohibit

**Exist**  accompanist analyst anarchist anthropologist
archeologist assist biologist Calvinist capitalist coexist
communist consist cyst desist dismissed egoist essayist
evangelist exorcist fatalist gist hissed humanist humorist
idealist imperialist insist journalist kissed list lobbyist
Methodist missed mist moralist motorist nationalist
novelist organist perfectionist pharmacist pianist plagiarist
psychologist romanticist satirist sentimentalist socialist
soloist specialist strategist terrorist theologist theorist
twist ventriloquist vocalist wrist

**Existed**  (see **Twisted**)

**Exotic**  chaotic erotic hypnotic idiotic macrobiotic narcotic
neurotic quixotic

**Expect**  (see **Effect**)

**Expense**  (see **Fence**)

**Expensive**  apprehensive comprehensive defensive extensive
incomprehensive inexpensive intensive offensive pensive

**Expert**  (see **Hurt**)

**Explain**  abstain again airplane arraign ascertain attain brain
Cain campaign cane chain champagne cocaine complain
contain crane detain disdain domain drain entertain
feign gain grain humane hurricane hydroplane insane
lane main Maine maintain mane migraine obtain ordain
pain pane pertain plain plane profane propane rain refrain
reign rein remain sane slain Spain sprain stain strain
sustain train vain vane vein wane windowpane

**Explode**  (see **Road**)

**Explore**  (see **Door**)

**Export**  (see **Court**)

**Exposure**  closure composure disclosure foreclosure

**Exterior**  inferior interior superior ulterior

**Extinction**  distinction

**Extortion**  abortion contortion extortion portion proportion

**Extreme**  beam cream deem dream esteem gleam ream
regime scheme scream seam seen steam stream supreme
team teem

**Eye**  alibi amplify banzai barfly butterfly buy by bye certify
clarify crucify cry defy deify deny die dignify diversify
dragonfly drive-by dry dye firefly fly fry glorify gratify
guy high horrify I identify imply July justify lie lullaby
modify my mystify notify passerby pie pry qualify rely
rye satisfy sci-fi shy sigh signify simplify sky sly specify
spry spy terrify testify thigh tie try underlie verify why

**Eyes**  (see **Lies**)

**E**

# F

**Fable** (see **Able**)

**Face** ace base bass brace case chase commonplace debase disgrace displace embrace encase erase grace lace mace misplace pace place race replace space steeplechase trace unlace vase

**Facial** glacial racial spatial

**Fact** (see **Act**)

**Factor** actor benefactor contractor detractor distracter extractor reactor refractor tractor

**Factory** refractory satisfactory (see *story, be*)

**Factual** actual contractual

**Fade** (see **Afraid**)

**Fail** ale bail bale blackmail braille cocktail curtail exhale female flail frail hail hale impale inhale jail mail male nail pale prevail rail regale sail sale scale shale snail stale tail they'll veil whale

**Faint** acquaint ain't complaint paint quaint restraint saint taint 'tain't

**Fair** (see **Air**)

**Fairy** (see **Cherry**)

**Fake** ache bake brake break cake flake forsake headache heartache keepsake make mistake opaque quake rake sake shake snake stake steak take wake

**Fall** all ball bawl brawl call crawl doll drawl gall haul install mall maul Montreal nightfall overhaul parasol pitfall protocol rainfall scrawl shawl small snowfall sprawl stall tall thrall wall waterfall y'all

**Fame** acclaim aim became blame came claim exclaim flame
frame game inflame lame maim name proclaim same
shame tame

**Family** (see **Be**)

**Famine** examine

**Famous** (see **Us**)

**F**

**Fantastic** bombastic drastic elastic enthusiastic gymnastic
iconoclastic plastic sarcastic scholastic spastic

**Fantasy** (see **Be**)

**Far** are bar bazaar bizarre car caviar cigar czar disbar guitar
jar par scar spar star tar

**Farce** parse sparse

**Farm** arm alarm charm disarm forearm harm

**Fashion** ashen bashin' compassion impassion passion

**Fast** aghast blast cast classed contrast flabbergast forecast
gassed last mast outlast overcast passed past vast

**Fat** (see **At**)

**Fatigue** intrigue league

**Fatty** batty catty chatty Cincinnati natty Patty ratty

**Fault** assault cobalt exalt halt malt salt somersault vault

**Favor** braver cadaver favor flavor graver paver saver savor
shaver waiver waver

**Fear** adhere appear atmosphere auctioneer beer bombardier
career cashier cavalier chandelier cheer clear dear deer
disappear ear engineer financier frontier gear hear
hemisphere here insincere interfere jeer lavaliere leer
mere mountaineer near overhear overseer peer
persevere pioneer queer racketeer reappear rear revere
seer severe shear sheer sincere smear sneer spear sphere
stratosphere tear veneer volunteer year

**Feast** beast ceased creased deceased east least pieced
    priest yeast

**Feat** (see **Sweet**)

**Feather** altogether Heather leather tether together weather
    whether (see *her*)

**Feature** bleacher creature preacher screecher teacher

**Fed** ahead bed bedspread bread bred coed dead dread
    figurehead fled flowerbed fountainhead gingerbread head
    inbred lead led misled misread overfed read red riverbed
    said shed shred sled sped spread thoroughbred thread
    underfed unthread wed

**F**

**Fee** (see **Be**)

**Feed** agreed bleed breed centipede concede creed deed
    exceed greed heed inbreed knead lead mislead need
    precede proceed read recede reed secede seed speed
    stampede succeed Swede tweed weed

**Feel** appeal automobile Bastille Camille conceal deal eel
    genteel he'll heal heel ideal kneel meal mobile peel real
    reel repeal reveal seal she'll spiel squeal steal steel veal
    we'll wheal zeal

**Feeling** appealing ceiling concealing congealing dealing healing
    kneeling pealing peeling reeling repealing revealing
    squealing stealing unfeeling wheeling

**Feet** (see **Sweet**)

**Feline** beeline sea-line (see *mine*)

**Fell** bell belle Carmel carrousel cell clientele dell dwell excel
    farewell gel hell hotel infidel knell mademoiselle personnel
    sell shell smell spell tell well yell

**Fellow** bellow cello hello mellow Othello yellow

**Felt** belt Celt dealt heartfelt melt pelt welt

**Female**  (see **Fail**)

**Feminine**  (see **Been**)

**Fence**  abstinence affluence benevolence circumference
coincidence commence competence condense
conference confidence consequence convenience defense
difference dispense dissidence eloquence evidence
excellence expense experience frankincense immense
impotence incense incidence incompetence indigence
influence innocence intense magnificence negligence
obedience permanence preference pretense reference
reverence sense suspense tense violence

**Fern**  (see **Learn**)

**Fertile**  girdle hurdle myrtle turtle

**Fetch**  catch etch kvetch retch sketch stretch wretch

**Feud**  allude altitude aptitude attitude delude dude fortitude
gratitude interlude latitude lewd longitude magnitude
multitude nude prelude pursued renewed solitude
subdued sued 'tude you'd

**Fever**  achiever beaver believer cleaver deceiver leave 'er
receiver reliever retriever weaver

**Few**  (see **Knew**)

**Fib**  ad lib crib glib rib

**Fiction**  addiction affliction benediction contradiction
conviction crucifixion depiction diction eviction friction
jurisdiction prediction restriction

**Fiddle**  diddle griddle middle riddle twiddle

**Field**  battlefield Chesterfield shield wield yield

**Fiend**  cleaned gleaned meaned quarantined weaned

**Fierce**  pierce

**Fiery**  (see **Be**)

F

**Fight**  (see **Flight**)

**Figment**  pigment

**File**  aisle awhile beguile bile compile crocodile defile isle
juvenile meanwhile mile Nile pile rile smile style tile vile
while wile worthwhile

**Fill**  bill chill daffodil distill drill frill fulfill gill grill hill ill imbecile
instill kill mill nil quill shrill sill skill spill still swill thrill till
trill until whippoorwill will windmill windowsill

**Final**  spinal vinyl

**Finance**  advance ants chance circumstance dance enhance
extravagance France glance lance pants prance romance
stance trance

**Fine**  align asinine assign benign combine concubine confine
consign decline define design dine divine entwine incline
line malign mine nine outshine pine porcupine recline
refine resign Rhine shine shrine sign spine stein swine
twine underline undermine vine whine wine

**Finger**  linger

**Finish**  diminish Finnish

**Fire**  acquire admire amplifier aspire attire buyer choir
conspire crier cryer desire dire drier dryer entire
esquire expire flier friar higher hire inquire inspire
justifier liar magnifier multiplier mystifier perspire prior
prophesier require retire satisfier sire squire supplier
testifier tire transpire wire

**Firm**  affirm confirm germ reaffirm sperm squirm term worm

**First**  burst cursed nursed outburst thirst versed worst

**Fish**  devilish dish gibberish impoverish squish swish wish

**Fishy**  squishy swishy

**Fit**  befit bit 'git grit kit knit hit it lit nit-wit pit quit sit spit
twit unfit wit zit

**F**

**Fix**  acrobatics bics crucifix fiddlesticks kicks licks
mathematics mix nix picks politics six sticks Styx
ticks transfix tricks wicks

**Fixture**  mixture

**Fizz**  biz friz his is quiz showbiz 'tis whiz

**Fizzle**  chisel drizzle frizzle grizzle sizzle swizzle

**F**

**Flag**  bag brag drag gag hag lag mag nag rag sag shag slag snag
stag swag tag wag

**Flannel**  channel panel

**Flap**  cap chap clap flap gap handicap lap map mishap nap rap
sap scrap slap snap strap tap trap wrap zap

**Flash**  ash balderdash bash brash cash clash crash dash gnash
rash rehash slash smash splash stash thrash trash

**Flat**  (see **At**)

**Flattery**  battery (see *be*)

**Flaunt**  daunt gaunt haunt jaunt taunt want

**Flea**  (see **Be**)

**Flesh**  enmesh fresh mesh refresh

**Flew**  (see **Do**)

**Flick**  (see **Kick**)

**Flight**  appetite bite blight bright byte contrite copyright
daylight delight despite dynamite excite Fahrenheit fight
fright headlight height ignite invite kite knight light
midnight might moonlight night outright parasite plight
polite quite recite reunite right satellite sight site sleight
slight spite starlight sunlight tight trite twilight unite
white write

**Flip**  battleship chip clip dip drip equip grip gyp hip lip nip quip
rip scrip ship slip snip strip tip trip whip zip

**Flirt**  alert avert blurt concert convert curt desert dessert
dirt divert exert expert extrovert insert introvert invert
pervert shirt skirt squirt subvert yogurt

**Float** (see **Boat**)

**Flock** (see **Clock**)

**Flood**   blood bud cud dud mud scud spud stud thud

**Floor**   abhor ambassador ashore auditor bachelor Baltimore before boar bore chancellor chore commodore competitor conspirator contributor core corps corridor deplore dinosaur door drawer Ecuador editor emperor encore evermore explore exterior folklore for fore four furthermore galore governor ignore implore inferior lore matador metaphor more nevermore nor oar offshore or orator ore poor pour rapport restore roar score seashore senator señor shore Singapore snore soar sophomore sore spore store swore therefore Thor tore troubadour underscore uproar visitor yore your

**Flop** (see **Drop**)

**Flour**   devour hour our scour (see *flower*)

**Flourish**   amateurish nourish

**Flow**   afro although banjo beau below bestow blow bow buffalo bungalow calico crossbow crow depot doe domino dough embryo escrow Eskimo foe forgo fro gazebo gigolo glow go grow heigh-ho ho-ho hobo hoe incognito indigo Joe know long ago low Mexico mistletoe mow no oboe oh outgrow overflow overgrow overthrow owe Pinocchio pistachio plateau quo rainbow ratio roe row sew slow snow so Soho status quo stow studio tally-ho though throw tiptoe to-and-fro toe Tokyo tow tremolo undergo undertow vertigo woe yo yo-yo

**Flower**   cauliflower cower deflower empower horsepower plower power shower tower (see *our*)

**Flowery**   bowery dowry floury flowery showery

F

**Flowing**  blowing bowing crowing glowing going growing hoeing
knowing mowing overflowing owing rowing sewing slowing
snowing sowing stowing throwing towing

**Flown**  (see **Known**)

**Fluffy**  huffy puffy stuffy

**Fluke**  kook spook

**F**

**Flunk**  bunk chunk clunk cyberpunk drunk dunk funk hunk
junk monk plunk punk shrunk skunk slunk spunk stunk
sunk trunk

**Flute**  (see **Cute**)

**Fly**  alibi amplify banzai barfly butterfly buy by bye certify clarify
crucify cry defy deify deny die dignify diversify dragonfly
drive-by dry dye eye firefly fry glorify gratify guy high
horrify I identify imply July justify lie lullaby modify my
mystify notify passerby pie pry qualify rely rye satisfy sci-
fi shy sigh signify simplify sky sly specify spry spy terrify
testify thigh tie try underlie verify why

**Focus**  hocus-pocus locus (see *us*)

**Foe**  (see **Blow**)

**Fog**  analog bog catalog clog cog demagogue dialogue dog
epilogue flog frog grog hog hot dog jog log monologue
prairie dog synagogue travelogue

**Foggy**  doggy froggy groggy soggy

**Foil**  broil coil loyal oil recoil royal spoil toil turmoil

**Fold**  behold blindfold bold centerfold cold foothold foretold
gold hold household marigold mold old retold scold sold
told uphold withhold

**Folk**  (see **Joke**)

**Follow**  Apollo hollow swallow wallow

**Folly**  collie dolly finale golly jolly melancholy Molly Polly
tamale trolley volley

**Fond**  beyond blond bond correspond dawned pond respond spawned vagabond wand yawned

**Food**  brood clued conclude crude dude exclude glued include intrude misconstrued mood preclude prude rude seclude shrewd wooed

**Fool**  April fool cool drool ghoul Liverpool overrule pool rule school spool stool tool whirlpool

**F**

**Foot**  afoot leadfoot pussyfoot tenderfoot put

**For**  (see **Door**)

**Forbid**  bid did grid hid invalid lid Madrid pyramid rid skid slid squid

**Ford**  (see **Lord**)

**Foreclosure**  closure composure disclosure exposure

**Forever**  clever endeavor ever however lever never sever whatever whenever wherever whoever

**Forge**  George gorge

**Forget**  alphabet bayonet bet brunette cabinet cadet cigarette clarinet cornet corvette debt duet epithet etiquette fret gazette get jet Joliet Juliet let luncheonette marionette met net omelet pet quartet regret roulette set silhouette Somerset sunset sweat threat Tibet toilette upset vet 'vette violet wet yet

**Forgiven**  driven given (see *in*)

**Forgotten**  begotten cotten gotten rotten

**Fork**  cork New York pork torque stork uncork

**Form**  chloroform conform deform inform norm perform rainstorm reform snowstorm storm swarm transform uniform warm

**Formal**  abnormal informal normal

**Fort**  (see **Court**)

**Forth** fourth henceforth north

**Fossil** apostle colossal docile jostle

**Fought** astronaut bought brought caught cosmonaut
fought naught ought overwrought sought taught
thought wrought

**Foul** cowl foul growl howl jowl owl prowl scowl waterfowl

**F**

**Found** abound around astound background battleground
bloodhound bound compound confound downed
dumbfound ground hound impound merry-go-round
mound pound profound renowned resound round sound
spellbound surround underground wound

**Foundry** boundary

**Fox** box chickenpox equinox mailbox orthodox ox paradox

**Fragile** agile (see *smile, fill*)

**Fragrance** flagrance vagrants

**Frantic** antic Atlantic chromatic gigantic pedantic
romantic transatlantic

**Fraternity** eternity maternity paternity

**Fraud** abroad applaud awed broad clod cod defraud façade
God guffawed Izod nod odd pod prod promenade quad
rod roughshod shod sod squad trod wad

**Freak** beak bleak creek eek leak meek reek seek speak
tweak weak week

**Freckle** heckle speckle

**Freeze** (see **Ease**)

**Frequence** sequence

**Fresh** enmesh flesh mesh refresh

**Friction** affliction benediction contradiction conviction
crucifixion depiction diction eviction fiction jurisdiction
prediction restriction

**Friend**　apprehend ascend attend befriend bend blend
　　　　commend comprehend condescend defend depend
　　　　descend dividend end expend extend fend intend lend
　　　　mend offend penned pretend recommend send spend
　　　　suspend tend transcend trend unbend

**Fright**　(see **Flight**)

**Frigid**　rigid

**Fringe**　binge cringe hinge infringe singe

**F**

**Frisky**　risky whiskey

**Frog**　analog bog catalog clog cog fog demagogue dialogue
　　　　dog epilogue frog grog hog jog log monologue
　　　　synagogue travelogue

**Front**　affront blunt brunt bunt confront forefront grunt hunt
　　　　punt runt shunt stunt

**Frost**　bossed cost crossed exhaust flossed holocaust lost
　　　　Pentecost tossed

**Frown**　brown clown crown down downtown drown frown
　　　　gown hand-me-down noun renown town tumble-down
　　　　upside down uptown

**Froze**　arose chose close compose decompose depose
　　　　disclose dispose doze enclose expose foreclose goes hose
　　　　impose indispose interpose knows nose owes pose
　　　　predispose presuppose prose recompose rose suppose
　　　　those toes transpose woes

**Frozen**　chosen dozin' mosin' nosin' posin'

**Fruit**　(see **Cute**)

**Frustrate**　(see **Ate**)

**Fry**　(see **Cry**)

**Fuel**　cruel duel jewel perusal renewal

**Fun**  anyone begun bun comparison done everyone Galveston
gun hon Hun jettison none nun oblivion one outdone
outrun overdone overrun phenomenon pun run shun
simpleton skeleton son stun sun ton unison venison won

**Function**  conjunction junction injunction

**Fund**  cummerbund refund rotund shunned

**Funky**  chunky flunky monkey spunky

**Funny**  bunny honey sunny

**Fur**  (see **Her**)

**Fury**  curry flurry hurry jury Missouri scurry slurry
surrey worry

**Fuss**  (see **Us**)

**Future**  suture

**Fuzz**  abuzz buzz cause coz does was

**F**

# G

**Gag**  bag brag drag flag hag lag mag nag rag sag shag slag snag stag swag tag wag

**Gain**  abstain again airplane arraign ascertain attain brain Cain campaign cane chain champagne cocaine complain contain crane detain disdain domain drain entertain explain feign grain humane hurricane hydroplane insane lane main Maine maintain mane migraine obtain ordain pain pane pertain plain plane profane propane rain refrain reign rein remain sane slain Spain sprain stain strain sustain train vain vane vein wane windowpane

**Gal**  canal chorale morale pal shall

**Galaxy**  (see **Be**)

**Gallery**  calorie Mallory salary

**Gamble**  amble ramble scramble shamble

**Garage**  barrage camouflage entourage mirage

**Garden**  harden pardon

**Gasoline**  (see **Mean**)

**Gasp**  asp clasp grasp

**Gave**  behave brave cave concave crave engrave forgave grave knave pave rave save shave slave waive wave

**Gavel**  gravel ravel travel unravel

**Gawk**  (see **Clock**)

**Gaze**  ablaze amaze appraise bays blaze braze craze days daze faze glaze graze haze malaise mayonnaise maze nays nowadays plays polonaise praise ways

**Geese**  cease crease decease decrease fleece grease Greece increase lease mantelpiece masterpiece peace piece police release

**Gem**  Bethlehem condemn hem phlegm requiem stem them

**Gender**  (see **Tender**)

**Generic**  atmospheric cleric Derrick esoteric hemispheric
  hysteric numeric

**Gentle**  accidental coincidental complemental compliment
  continental dental departmental detrimental
  experimental fundamental governmental incidental
  intercontinental lentil mental monumental Oriental
  parental regimental rental rudimental sentimental
  supplemental temperamental

**Gently**  evidently impotently innocently insolently intently

**Germ**  affirm confirm firm reaffirm sperm squirm term worm

**Get**  alphabet bayonet bet brunette cabinet cadet cigarette
  clarinet cornet corvette debt duet epithet etiquette
  forget fret gazette jet Joliet Juliet let luncheonette
  marionette met net omelet pet quartet regret roulette
  set silhouette Somerset sunset sweat threat Tibet toilette
  upset vet 'vette violet wet yet

**Ghetto**  allegretto amoretto falsetto libretto stiletto

**Ghost**  boast coast foremost furthermost host innermost
  most post roast toast whipping post

**Giant**  client compliant defiant reliant self-reliant

**Gift**  drift lift shift spendthrift swift thrift

**Giggle**  jiggle squiggle wiggle wriggle

**Gigolo**  bolo piccolo polo solo tremolo

**Gin**  aspirin been begin Berlin bin chagrin chin discipline
  feminine fin genuine grin harlequin heroine in inn kin
  mandolin mannequin masculine moccasin origin pin
  saccharine shin sin skin spin thick-and-thin thin tin twin
  violin win within

**G**

**Ginger**  injure infringer

**Girl**  curl earl hurl pearl swirl twirl whirl

**Give**  affirmative alternative argumentative combative competitive consecutive conservative definitive expletive figurative forgive fugitive informative intuitive live lucrative narrative negative positive primitive prohibitive provocative relative representative sensitive talkative tentative

**Glad**  ad add bad Brad cad Chad clad Dad egad fad grad had lad mad nomad pad plaid sad shad Trinidad

**G**

**Glamorous**  amorous clamorous (see *us*)

**Glamour**  clamor damn 'er grammar hammer slammer sledgehammer stammer yammer

**Glance**  advance ants chance circumstance dance enhance extravagance finance France lance pants prance romance stance trance

**Glass**  (see **Class**)

**Glitter**  bitter counterfeiter critter fitter fritter litter quitter sitter transmitter twitter (see *her*)

**Gloat**  (see **Boat**)

**Globe**  disrobe Job probe robe strobe

**Gloom**  bloom boom broom cloakroom doom entomb flume groom room tomb whom womb zoom

**Glorify**  horrify

**Glory**  accusatory allegory category dormitory dory gory hunky-dory laboratory Lori obligatory observatory oratory Peter Lorre quarry reformatory retaliatory sorry story territory Tory

**Glove**  above dove ladylove love mourning dove of shove turtle dove

**Glow**  afro although banjo beau below bestow blow bow
buffalo bungalow calico crossbow crow depot doe
domino dough embryo escrow Eskimo flow foe forgo
fro gazebo gigolo go grow heigh ho ho-ho hobo hoe
incognito indigo Joe know long-ago low Mexico mistletoe
mow no oboe oh outgrow overflow overgrow overthrow
owe Pinocchio pistachio plateau quo rainbow ratio roe
row sew slow snow so Soho status quo stow studio
tally-ho though throw tiptoe to-and-fro toe Tokyo tow
tremolo undergo undertow vertigo woe yo yo-yo

**Glue**  (see **Do**)

**Glum**  album aquarium auditorium become bum burdensome
Christendom come cranium crematorium crumb
curriculum drum dumb emporium fee-fi-fo-fum gum
gymnasium hum kettledrum kingdom martyrdom
maximum meddlesome medium millennium minimum
mum museum numb opium overcome pendulum
petroleum platinum plum premium quarrelsome radium
random rum sanitarium scum slum some strum succumb
sum swum tedium thumb Tom Thumb Tweedledum
uranium worrisome yum

**Glut**  (see **But**)

**Gnarl**  Carl snarl

**Go**  afro although banjo beau below bestow blow bow buffalo
bungalow calico crossbow crow depot doe domino dough
embryo escrow Eskimo flow foe forgo fro gazebo gigolo
glow grow heigh ho ho-ho hobo hoe incognito indigo
Joe know long-ago low Mexico mistletoe mow no oboe
oh outgrow overflow overgrow overthrow owe Pinocchio
pistachio plateau quo rainbow ratio roe row sew slow

**G**

snow so Soho status quo stow studio tally-ho though throw tiptoe to-and-fro toe Tokyo tow tremolo undergo undertow vertigo woe yo yo-yo

**Goal**  (see **Hole**)

**God**  abroad applaud awed broad clod cod defraud façade fraud guffawed Izod nod odd pod prod promenade quad rod roughshod shod sod squad trod wad

**Goggle**  boggle boondoggle toggle

**Gold**  behold blindfold bold centerfold cold fold foothold foretold hold household marigold mold old retold scold sold told uphold withhold

**Golly**  collie dolly finale folly jolly melancholy Molly Polly tamale trolley volley

**Gone**  Amazon autobahn Babylon bonbon Bonn brawn chiffon con dawn drawn echelon fawn lawn neon on pawn pentagon silicon swan undergone upon wan woebegone wonton yawn

**Good**  brotherhood could fatherhood firewood Hollywood hood likelihood livelihood misunderstood motherhood neighborhood should sisterhood stood understood withstood womanhood wood would

**Goose**  caboose loose moose noose papoose recluse spruce truce vamoose

**Gorilla**  guerrilla Manila Priscilla vanilla villa

**Gory**  (see **Story**)

**Gown**  (see **Clown**)

**Grab**  blab cab crab dab drab gab jab lab nab scab slab stab tab

**Grace**  ace  base bass brace case chase commonplace debase disgrace displace embrace encase erase face lace mace misplace pace place race replace space steeplechase trace unlace vase

**Grade**  aid arcade afraid barricade blade blockade braid
brayed brigade centigrade charade crusade degrade
dismayed dissuade downgrade escapade evade fade
grenade hayed invade laid lemonade made maid paid
parade persuade played promenade raid renegade serenade
shade spade stockade suede tirade trade

**Grain**  (see **Insane**)

**Gram**  (see **Am**)

**G**

**Granny**  Annie canny fanny nanny

**Grape**  ape cape cityscape drape escape landscape seascape
shape tape

**Graph**  calf carafe epitaph giraffe paragraph phonograph
photograph polygraph riffraff staff telegraph

**Grasp**  asp clasp gasp

**Grass**  alas amass ass bass brass class crass gas glass harass
hourglass lass looking-glass mass morass mustache
overpass pass sass sassafras surpass

**Gratitude**  attitude latitude platitude

**Grave**  behave brave cave concave crave engrave forgave gave
knave pave rave save shave slave waive wave

**Gravel**  gavel ravel travel unravel

**Gravity**  cavity depravity

**Greed**  agreed breed centipede concede creed deed exceed
feed heed inbreed knead lead mislead need precede
proceed read recede reed secede seed speed stampede
succeed Swede tweed weed

**Greedy**  beady needy seedy speedy weedy (see *be*)

**Green**  (see **Mean**)

**Greet**  athlete beat beet bittersweet bleat cheat compete
complete conceit concrete deceit defeat delete deplete
discreet discrete eat elite feat feet fleet heat incomplete

indiscreet meat meet mistreat neat obsolete parakeet
receipt repeat retreat seat sheet sleet street suite sweet
treat wheat

**Grew**  (see **Do**)

**Grief**  beef belief brief chief disbelief leaf relief thief

**Grieve**  achieve believe bereave conceive disbelieve eve
heave leave perceive receive relieve reprieve retrieve
sleeve weave

**Grill**  bill chill daffodil distill drill fill frill fulfill gill hill ill imbecile
instill kill mill nil quill shrill sill skill spill still swill thrill till
trill until whippoorwill will windmill windowsill

**Grim**  brim dim gym him hymn limb pseudonym skim slim
swim trim whim

**Grin**  aspirin been begin Berlin bin chagrin chin discipline
feminine fin genuine gin harlequin heroine in inn kin
mandolin mannequin masculine moccasin origin pin
saccharine shin sin skin spin thick-and-thin thin tin twin
violin win within

**Grip**  (see **Trip**)

**Grocer**  closer (see *sir*)

**Groin**  coin Des Moines join loin purloin sirloin tenderloin

**Gross**  adios bellicose close comatose diagnose dose engross
grandiose morose nose overdose varicose verbose

**Grouch**  couch crouch ouch pouch slouch vouch

**Ground**  (see **Found**)

**Group**  coop droop dupe hoop loop nincompoop poop scoop
sloop soup stoop swoop troop troupe whoop

**Grovel**  hovel novel

**Grow**  (see **Glow**)

**Grown**  (see **Known**)

**Growth**  both loath oath overgrowth undergrowth

**Guard** avant-garde card chard discard disregard hard lard
regard retard tarred yard

**Guess** access address baroness bashfulness bitterness bless
caress chess cleverness cloudiness compress confess
craziness deadliness depress digress distress dizziness
dress duress eagerness easiness eeriness emptiness
excess express finesse foolishness ghostliness happiness
haziness homelessness idleness impress joyfulness
joylessness laziness less limitless Loch Ness lustfulness
mess nervousness obsess openness oppress
outrageousness penniless playfulness possess press
profess progress queasiness recess regress repossess
repress rockiness seediness shallowness silkiness
sleaziness sleepiness sneakiness SOS spaciousness
spitefulness stress success suppress thoughtfulness
transgress uselessness viciousness willingness wishfulness
worldliness yes youthfulness

**Guest** (see **Best**)

**Guilt** built hilt jilt kilt quilt spilt stilt tilt Vanderbilt wilt

**Guitar** are bar bazaar bizarre car caviar cigar czar disbar far
jar par scar spar star tar

**Gulch** mulch

**Gull** annul cull dull hull lull mull scull skull

**Gum** (see **Dumb**)

**Gun** anyone begun bun comparison done everyone fun
Galveston hon Hun jettison none nun oblivion one
outdone outrun overdone overrun phenomenon pun
run shun simpleton skeleton son stun sun ton unison
venison won

**G**

**Guppy**  puppy yuppie

**Gust**  (see **Trust**)

**Gut**  but butt cut glut halibut hut King Tut mutt nut putt rut
scuttlebutt shut smut strut uncut

**Gutter**  butter clutter cutter flutter mutter putter shutter
sputter strutter stutter utter

**Guy**  alibi amplify banzai barfly butterfly buy by bye certify
clarify crucify defy deify deny die dignify diversify
dragonfly drive-by dry dye eye firefly fly fry glorify gratify
high horrify I identify imply July justify lie lullaby modify
my mystify notify passerby pie pry qualify rely rye satisfy
sci-fi shy sigh signify simplify sky sly specify spry spy terrify
testify thigh tie try underlie verify why

**Gypsy**  dipsy Poughkeepsie tipsy

**G**

# H

**Had**  ad add bad Brad cad Chad clad Dad egad fad glad grad
   lad mad nomad pad plaid sad shad Trinidad

**Hail**  (see **Ale**)

**Hair**  (see **Air**)

**Hairy**  carry hari-kari marry miscarry parry vary (see *cherry*)

**Hallow**  callow fallow mallow marshmallow shallow tallow

**Halloween**  (see **Mean**)

**Halt**  assault cobalt exalt fault malt salt somersault vault

**Hammer**  clamor damn 'er glamour grammar slammer
   sledgehammer stammer yammer

**Hand**  and band brand canned command contraband demand
   expand fanned grand land panned planned reprimand Rio
   Grande sand stand

**Handle**  candle dandle sandal scandal vandal

**Handy**  Andy brandy candy dandy randy sandy

**Hanky**  cranky lanky Yankee

**Happiness**  (see **Guess**)

**Happy**  crappie nappy pappy sappy scrappy slaphappy yappy

**Harbor**  arbor barber (see *door*)

**Hard**  avant-garde card chard discard disregard guard lard
   regard retard tarred yard

**Hark**  aardvark arc ark bark dark embark lark mark narc park
   patriarch remark shark spark stark

**Harm**  arm alarm charm disarm farm forearm

**Harmonic**  catatonic chronic diatonic enharmonic ironic
   monophonic philharmonic phonic platonic polyphonic
   sonic symphonic tonic

**Harmonica**  Monica Santa Monica Veronica

**Harp**  carp sharp

**Harsh**  marsh

**Has**  as jazz razzmatazz whereas

**Haste**  baste aftertaste braced chaste distaste faced freckle-
     faced hatchet-faced lambaste paste taste waist waste

**Hat**  (see **At**)

**Hatch**  attach batch catch detach dispatch latch match patch
     scratch snatch

**Hatchet**  latchet ratchet

**Hate**  (see **Ate**)

**Hated**  anticipated bated belated dated fated grated mated
     rated related sedated skated x-rated (see **Ate(d)**)

**H**

**Haunt**  daunt flaunt gaunt jaunt taunt want

**Haunting**  daunting flaunting jaunting taunting
     vaunting wanting

**Have**  calve

**Hawk**  (see **Clock**)

**Haze**  ablaze amaze appraise bays blaze braze craze days daze
     faze gaze glaze graze malaise mayonnaise maze nays
     nowadays plays polonaise praise ways

**Hazel**  appraisal nasal

**Hazy**  crazy daisy lazy

**He**  (see **Be**)

**Head**  ahead bed bedspread bread bred coed dead dread fed
     figurehead fled flowerbed fountainhead gingerbread inbred
     lead led misled misread overfed read red riverbed said
     shed shred sled sped spread thoroughbred thread
     underfed unthread wed

**Heal**  appeal automobile Bastille Camille conceal deal eel feel
     genteel he'll heel ideal kneel meal mobile peel real reel
     repeal reveal seal she'll spiel squeal steal steel veal we'll
     wheal zeal

**Healer** congealer dealer feeler reeler sealer squealer
   stealer wheeler

**Health** commonwealth stealth wealth

**Hear** (see **Near**)

**Heard** absurd bird blackbird bluebird curd herd hummingbird
   ladybird mockingbird overheard third word yellowbird

**Hearse** adverse converse curse disburse disperse diverse
   immerse intersperse inverse nurse purse rehearse
   reverse terse transverse traverse universe verse worse

**H**

**Heart** apart art cart chart counterpart dart depart mart part
   smart start sweetheart tart upstart

**Heartache** (see **Ache**)

**Heat** (see **Sweet**)

**Heaven** eleven leaven seven

**Heavy** bevy Chevy levee

**Heck** check Czech deck fleck neck peck Quebec speck
   trek wreck

**Height** (see **Flight**)

**Heist** Christ diced feist iced zeitgeist

**Held** felled meld upheld weld

**Hell** bell belle Carmel carrousel cell clientele dell dwell excel
   farewell fell gel hotel infidel knell mademoiselle personnel
   sell shell smell spell tell well yell

**Hellbound** hellhound spellbound (see *found*)

**Hellfire** shellfire (see *fire*)

**Hellish** embellish relish

**Hello** bellow cello fellow mellow Othello yellow

**Help** kelp yelp

**Her** amateur blur chauffeur concur confer connoisseur
   defer demur deter fur incur infer Jennifer myrrh occur
   per prefer purr recur sir slur spur stir transfer voyageur
   were whir

**Hercules**  (see **Ease**)

**Here**  (see **Near**)

**Hero**  Nero zero (see *know*)

**Hesitative**  (see **Native**)

**Hey**  (see **Say**)

**Hid**  bid did forbid grid invalid lid Madrid pyramid rid skid
  slid squid

**Hide**  beside bonafide bride collide confide countryside decide
  defied died dignified divide eyed fireside guide hillside
  homicide inside lied outside override pride provide reside
  ride side slide snide stride subdivide subside suicide tide
  tried wide yuletide

**High**  (see **Cry**)

**Highlight**  skylight twilight (see *light*)

**Highway**  byway skyway (see *way*)

**Hijacker**  attacker backer blacker cracker hacker nutcracker
  packer ransacker slacker smacker tracker

**Hike**  bike like mike spike strike tyke

**Hilarious**  Aquarius gregarious precarious Sagittarius
  various (see *us*)

**Hill**  (see **Fill**)

**Hilly**  Billy Chile Chili chilly dilly filly frilly hillbilly lily Philly
  Piccadilly piccalilli shrilly silly willy-nilly

**Him**  brim dim grim gym hymn limb pseudonym skim slim
  swim trim whim

**Hinge**  binge cringe fringe infringe singe

**Hint**  flint lint mint peppermint print spearmint splint sprint
  squint tint

**Hip**  (see **Trip**)

**Hippie**  chippy dippy drippy flippy Mississippi nippy slippy
  snippy tippy yippee zippy

**Hire**  (see **Fire**)

**H**

**His** biz fizz friz is quiz showbiz 'tis whiz

**Hiss** abyss amiss analysis armistice bliss carcass cowardice
dismiss emphasis hypothesis kiss miss nemesis office
prejudice Swiss synthesis this

**History** mystery (see *be*)

**Hit** befit bit fit 'git grit kit knit it lit nit-wit pit quit sit twit
unfit wit zit

**Hoagie** Bogie stogie

**Hoard** (see **Lord**)

**Hoax** chokes coax folks jokes polks smokes spokes yokes

**Hobby** bobby knobby lobby snobby (see *be*)

**Hold** behold blindfold bold centerfold cold fold foothold
foretold gold household marigold mold old retold scold
sold told uphold withhold

**Hole** bowl buttonhole cajole casserole coal control dole droll
enroll goal loophole Maypole mole Old King Cole oriole
parole patrol pole poll porthole role roll scroll tadpole
toll troll whole

**Holiday** (see **Say**)

**Hollow** Apollo follow swallow wallow

**Hollywood** (see **Good**)

**Holy** drolly lowly roly-poly solely wholly

**Home** chrome chromosome comb dome foam gnome
honeycomb metronome Nome poem roam Rome tome

**Honesty** (see **Be**)

**Honey** bunny funny money sunny

**Honolulu** Lulu Zulu

**Honor** dishonor goner

**Hood** (see **Good**)

**Hook** book brook cook crook look mistook nook outlook
rook shook took undertook

**Hoop**  coop droop dupe group loop nincompoop poop scoop
　　　sloop soup stoop swoop troop troupe whoop

**Hope**  antelope cantaloupe cope dope elope envelope grope
　　　gyroscope horoscope kaleidoscope microscope mope
　　　pope rope scope slope soap stethoscope telescope

**Horn**  adorn airborne born Cape Horn Capricorn corn
　　　lovelorn Matterhorn morn mourn popcorn scorn
　　　stillborn sworn unicorn warn worn

**Horny**  corny thorny

**Horrify**  glorify

**Horror**  adorer explorer gorer ignorer restorer roarer
　　　snorer soarer (see *her*)

**Horse**  coarse course divorce endorse force Norse reinforce
　　　remorse resource source

**Hosanna**  (see **Nirvana**)

**Host**  boast coast foremost furthermost ghost innermost
　　　most post roast toast whipping post

**Hot**  apricot blot Camelot clot cot cybot dot forget-me-not
　　　forgot fought gavotte got hot-shot jot knot lot not plot
　　　pot robot rot shot slingshot somewhat spot squat swat
　　　tot trot watt what yacht

**Hotel**  bell belle Carmel carrousel cell clientele dell dwell
　　　excel farewell fell gel hell infidel knell mademoiselle
　　　personnel sell shell smell spell tell well yell

**Hound**  abound around astound background battleground
　　　bloodhound bound compound confound downed
　　　dumbfound found ground impound merry-go-round
　　　mound pound profound renowned resound round sound
　　　spellbound surround underground wound

**Hour**  devour flour our scour (see *flower*)

**House**  blouse douse grouse louse madhouse mouse
　　　outhouse penthouse slaughterhouse souse spouse

**How** allow avow bough bow brow chow cow disavow endow
frau kowtow now ow plough plow row slough somehow
sow thou vow wow

**Howl** cowl foul fowl growl jowl owl prowl scowl waterfowl

**Huff** (see **Bluff**)

**Hug** bug drug dug jug lug mug plug pug rug shrug slug smug
snug thug tug

**Huge** centrifuge Scrooge stooge

**Hulk** bulk sulk

**Human** Harry S. Truman Paul Newman (see *man*)

**Humble** bumble crumble fumble grumble humble jumble
mumble rumble stumble tumble

**Humiliate** affiliate conciliate

**Humor** bloomer boomer consumer rumor tumor

**Hung** (see **Young**)

**Hunger** fishmonger rumormonger younger (see *her*)

**Hunt** affront blunt brunt bunt confront forefront front grunt
punt runt shunt stunt

**Hurdle** curdle girdle

**Hurricane** (see **Insane**)

**Hurry** curry flurry fury jury Missouri scurry slurry
surrey worry

**Hurt** alert avert blurt concert convert curt desert dessert
dirt divert exert expert extrovert flirt insert introvert
invert pervert shirt skirt squirt subvert yogurt

**Hustle** bustle corpuscle muscle mussel rustle tussle

**Hype** archetype gripe pipe prototype ripe stereotype stripe
swipe type wipe

**Hysteric** atmospheric cleric Derrick esoteric generic
hemispheric hysteric numeric

# I

**I** alibi amplify banzai barfly butterfly buy by bye certify clarify
crucify cry defy deify deny die dignify diversify dragonfly
drive-by dry dye eye firefly fly fry glorify gratify guy high
horrify I identify imply July justify lie lullaby modify my
mystify notify passerby pie pry qualify rely rye satisfy
sci-fi shy sigh signify simplify sky sly specify spry spy
terrify testify thigh tie try underlie verify why

**Ice** advice concise device dice entice lice mice nice paradise
precise price rice sacrifice spice splice suffice thrice
twice vice

**Icicle** bicycle tricycle

**Icy** dicey spicy

**Idealist** (see **Exist**)

**Idiot** (see **It**)

**Idol** bridal bridle homicidal idle suicidal tidal

**If** cliff handkerchief sniff stiff tiff whiff

**Iffy** jiffy sniffy spiffy

**Ignore** (see **Door**)

**Ill** bill chill daffodil distill drill fill frill fulfill gill grill hill imbecile
instill kill mill nil quill shrill sill skill spill still swill thrill till
trill until whippoorwill will windmill windowsill

**Illusion** allusion conclusion confusion delusion fusion
inclusion infusion seclusion transfusion

**Image** scrimmage

**Imitative** (see **Native**)

**Immature** (see **Cure**)

**Impostor** accoster foster lost 'er roster

**Impressive** aggressive depressive digressive excessive
expressive possessive progressive regressive successive

**In**  aspirin been begin Berlin bin chagrin chin discipline
feminine fin genuine gin grin harlequin heroine inn kin
mandolin mannequin masculine moccasin origin pin
saccharine shin sin skin spin thick-and-thin thin tin twin
violin win within

**Inch**  cinch flinch lynch pinch

**Include**  brood clued conclude crude dude exclude food
glued intrude misconstrued mood preclude prude rude
seclude shrewd wooed

**Increase**  cease crease decease decrease fleece geese grease
Greece lease mantelpiece masterpiece peace piece
police release

**Independent**  ascendant attendant defendant dependent
descendant independent pendant superintendent
transcendent

**Individual**  residual

**Indulge**  bulge divulge

**Industry**  (see **Be**)

**Infatuate**  (see **Ate**)

**Inferior**  exterior interior superior ulterior

**Infernal**  colonel eternal external fraternal internal journal
kernel maternal nocturnal paternal

**Inflict**  addict conflict constrict contradict convict derelict
evict flicked licked predict pricked strict

**Influence**  (see **Fence**)

**Influential**  confidential credential deferential differential
essential existential nonessential potential preferential
presidential providential prudential quintessential
residential sequential torrential

**Inherit**  demerit disinherit (see *it*)

**Initial**  artificial beneficial judicial official sacrificial superficial

I

**Injure**  ginger infringer

**Injury**  (see **Be**)

**Ink**  blink brink chink clink drink fink kink link mink pink rink
shrink sink slink stink wink zinc

**Innuendo**  crescendo diminuendo Nintendo (see *know*)

**Insane**  abstain again airplane arraign ascertain attain brain
Cain campaign cane chain champagne cocaine complain
contain crane detain disdain domain drain entertain
explain feign gain grain humane hurricane hydroplane
lane main Maine maintain mane migraine obtain ordain
pain pane pertain plain plane profane propane rain refrain
reign rein remain sane slain Spain sprain stain strain
sustain train vain vane vein wane windowpane

**Insecure**  (see **Cure**)

**Insert**  (see **Hurt**)

**Insist**  accompanist analyst anarchist anthropologist
archeologist assist biologist Calvinist capitalist coexist
communist consist cyst desist dismissed egoist essayist
evangelist exist exorcist fatalist gist hissed humanist
humorist idealist imperialist journalist kissed list lobbyist
Methodist missed mist moralist motorist nationalist
novelist organist perfectionist pharmacist pianist plagiarist
psychologist romanticist satirist sentimentalist socialist
soloist specialist strategist terrorist theologist theorist
twist ventriloquist vocalist wrist

**Insisted**  (see **Twisted**)

**Inspector**  collector connector deflector detector director
injector nectar objector projector prospector protector
reflector selector vector (see *her*)

**Inspiration**  congregational creational educational
recreational sensational

**Inspire** acquire admire amplifier aspire attire buyer choir
conspire crier cryer desire dire drier dryer entire esquire
expire fire flier friar higher hire inquire justifier liar
magnifier multiplier mystifier perspire prior prophesier
require retire satisfier sire squire supplier testifier tire
transpire wire

**Insurance** assurance endurance

**Intensive** apprehensive comprehensive defensive expensive
extensive incomprehensive inexpensive offensive pensive

**Invasion** abrasion dissuasion equation evasion
occasion persuasion

**Invent** (see **Bent**)

**Invention** (see **Tension**)

**Inventive** attentive inattentive incentive retentive

**Inventor** center dissenter enter experimenter frequenter
mentor presenter preventer renter tormenter

**Invest** arrest attest best breast chest congest crest detest
digest divest double-breast infest ingest interest jest
manifest molest nest protest quest request rest single-
breast suggest test vest

**Invisible** divisible indivisible visible

**Invite** appetite bite blight bright byte contrite copyright
daylight delight despite dynamite excite Fahrenheit fight
flight fright headlight height ignite kite knight light
midnight might moonlight night outright parasite plight
polite quite recite reunite right satellite sight site sleight
slight spite starlight sunlight tight trite twilight unite
white write

**Involve** absolve devolve dissolve evolve revolve solve

**Irate** gyrate (see *rate*)

**Ironic**  catatonic chronic diatonic enharmonic harmonic
     monophonic philharmonic phonic platonic polyphonic
     sonic symphonic tonic

**Is**  biz fizz friz his quiz showbiz 'tis whiz

**Island**  highland (see *land*)

**Issue**  tissue (see *you*)

**It**  befit bit fit 'git grit kit knit hit idiot lit nit-wit pit quit sit twit
     unfit wit zit

**Ivory**  (see **Be**)

I

# J

**Jacket**  bracket packet racket (see *it*)

**Jail**  ale bail bale blackmail braille cocktail curtail exhale fail female flail frail hail hale impale inhale mail male nail pale prevail rail regale sail sale scale shale snail stale tail they'll veil whale

**Jam**  (see **Am**)

**Jar**  are bar bazaar bizarre car caviar cigar czar disbar far guitar par scar spar star tar

**Jaw**  Arkansas awe bra caw claw draw flaw gnaw guffaw hurrah jaw law Ma macaw nah overdraw Pa paw raw saw seesaw shah slaw squaw straw thaw withdraw

**Jazz**  as has razzmatazz whereas

**Jealous**  tell us zealous (see **Us**)

**Jealousy**  (see **Be**)

**Jelly**  belly deli Kelly Shelly smelly

**Jerk**  clerk handiwork irk Kirk lurk murk overwork perk quirk shirk smirk Turk work

**Jester**  Chester contester fester investor Lester molester pester protester semester sequester tester Westchester Winchester

**Jet**  (see **Met**)

**Jewel**  cruel duel fuel

**Jiggle**  giggle squiggle wiggle wriggle

**Jingle**  intermingle Kris Kringle mingle shingle single tingle

**Jinx**  lynx minks sphinx thinks winks

**Job**  blob bob cob fob gob hob hobnob job knob lob mob nob rob slob snob sob swab throb

**Jock** Bangkok beanstalk boondock clock cock cornstalk crock
deadlock defrock dock flintlock flock frock gawk gridlock
hawk hock J. S. Bach knock Little Rock livestock lock
mock Mohawk padlock peacock rock shock sidewalk
small talk smock sock squawk stalk stock talk tomahawk
unlock walk wok

**Joe** (see **Glow**)

**Join** adjoin coin Des Moines groin loin purloin
sirloin tenderloin

**Joint** anoint appoint counterpoint disappoint disjoint

**Joke** artichoke baroque bloke broke choke cloak coke croak
evoke folk invoke oak poke provoke revoke smoke soak
spoke stroke toke woke yoke

**Joker** broker choker mediocre poker provoker revoker
smoker stoker stroker woke 'er

**Jolly** collie dolly finale folly golly melancholy Molly Polly
tamale trolley volley

**Jolt** bolt colt dolt revolt thunderbolt

**Journal** colonel eternal external fraternal infernal internal
kernel maternal nocturnal paternal

**Journalist** (see **Exist**)

**Journey** attorney tourney (see *be*)

**Joy** ahoy annoy boy buoy convoy corduroy coy decoy destroy
employ enjoy Illinois ploy Roy Savoy soy toy troy viceroy

**Judge** budge drudge fudge grudge misjudge nudge smudge

**Juggle** smuggle snuggle struggle

**Juice** (see **Abuse**)

**Jumbo** gumbo (see *no*)

**Jump** bump chump clump dump hump lump plump rump
slump stump thump trump ump

**Junction** conjunction function injunction

**June** attune commune dune immune impugn inopportune
tune (see *moon*)

**Jungle** bungle

**Junk** bunk chunk clunk cyberpunk drunk dunk flunk funk
hunk monk plunk punk shrunk skunk slunk spunk stunk
sunk trunk

**Juror** deferrer demurrer furor incurrer stirrer (see *her*)

**Jury** curry flurry fury hurry Missouri scurry slurry
surrey worry

**Just** adjust August bust crust disgust distrust encrust entrust
gust lust mistrust must robust rust thrust trust unjust

**J**

**Juvenile** (see **Smile**)

# K

**Keep** barkeep cheep creep deep heap leap peep reap seep
   sheep sleep steep sweep weep

**Keg** beg egg leg peg

**Kept** accept adept crept except intercept overslept slept
   stepped swept wept

**Key** (see **Be**)

**Kick** arithmetic arsenic brick candlestick candlewick
   Catholic chick click flick heartsick hick lick limerick
   love-sick lunatic maverick nick pick sick slick stick
   thick tic tick wick

**Kid** bid did forbid grid hid invalid lid Madrid pyramid rid
   skid slid squid

**Kill** (see **Fill**)

**Killer** caterpillar chiller distiller driller filler instiller pillar
   shriller spiller swiller thriller tiller

**Killing** (see **Willing**)

**Kin** aspirin been begin Berlin bin chagrin chin discipline
   feminine fin genuine gin grin harlequin heroine in inn
   mandolin mannequin masculine moccasin origin pin
   saccharine shin sin skin spin thick-and-thin thin tin twin
   violin win within

**Kind** behind bind blind find grind hind humankind mastermind
   mind remind signed unkind unwind wind wined

**Kindle** dwindle rekindle spindle swindle

**King** anything bring cling ding evening everything fling ring
   sing sling spring sting string swing thing wing wring (add
   "ing" to "action" words, i.e., run(ning), etc.)

**Kingdom** (see **Dumb**)

**K**

**Kinky** blinky dinky pinky slinky stinky

**Kiss** abyss amiss analysis armistice carcass cowardice dismiss
emphasis hiss hypothesis miss nemesis office prejudice
Swiss synthesis this

**Kissing** dismissing 'dissing hissing missing reminiscing

**Kit** befit bit fit 'git grit knit hit idiot it lit nit-wit pit quit sit
twit unfit wit zit

**Kitten** bitten Briton mitten smitten written (see *in*)

**Kitty** city committee ditty gritty pity pretty self-pity witty

**Knee** (see **Be**)

**Knew** adieu anew avenue barbecue bayou chew choo-choo
cue curfew debut dew due ensue ewe few guru
honeydew hue I.O.U. imbue ingénue interview Jew lieu
new Nehru overdue pee-ewe pew preview pursue renew
residue revenue review spew subdue sue undue view yew
you (see *do*)

**Knight** (see **Light**)

**Knife** afterlife jackknife life strife wife

**Knob** blob bob cob fob gob hob hobnob job lob mob nob
rob slob snob sob swab throb

**Knock** (see **Clock**)

**Knot** apricot blot Camelot clot cot cybot dot forget-me-
not forgot fought gavotte got hot hot-shot jot lot not
plot pot robot rot shot slingshot somewhat spot squat
swat tot trot watt what yacht

**Know** afro although banjo beau below bestow blow bow
buffalo bungalow calico crossbow crow depot doe
domino dough embryo escrow Eskimo flow foe forgo
fro gazebo gigolo glow go grow heigh ho ho-ho hobo hoe
incognito indigo Joe long-ago low Mexico mistletoe

**K**

mow no oboe oh outgrow overflow overgrow overthrow
owe Pinocchio pistachio plateau quo rainbow ratio roe
row sew slow snow so Soho status quo stow studio
tally-ho though throw tiptoe to-and-fro toe Tokyo tow
tremolo undergo undertow vertigo woe yo yo-yo

**Knowledge** acknowledge college (see *ledge*)

**Known** alone atone backbone baritone blown bone
chaperone clone condone cone cornerstone cyclone
Dictaphone flown full-blown full-grown gramophone
grindstone groan grown headstone loan lone microphone
milestone moan monotone mown overgrown overthrown
own phone postpone prone saxophone sewn shown
stone telephone thrown tone trombone unknown
xylophone zone

**Knuckle** arbuckle buckle chuckle honeysuckle suckle

**Koran** an ban can can-can Dan fan Iran man Nan plan Tehran

**Kosher** so sure  (see *her*)

**K**

# L

**Lab** blab cab crab dab drab gab grab jab nab scab slab stab tab

**Label** (see **Able**)

**Labor** belabor neighbor saber

**Lack** almanac attack back black bric-a-brac Cadillac cardiac
clickety-clack egomaniac feedback hack Hackensack
haystack jack kleptomaniac knack maniac pack plaque
Pontiac prozac quack rack sack shack slack snack stack
tack track whack yak zodiac

**Lad** (see **Mad**)

**Lamp** amp camp champ clamp cramp damp ramp stamp vamp

**Land** and band brand canned command contraband demand
expand fanned grand hand panned planned reprimand Rio
Grande sand stand

**Lane** (see **Rain**)

**Large** barge charge discharge enlarge

**Lark** aardvark arc ark bark dark embark hark mark narc park
patriarch remark shark spark stark

**Laser** appraiser blazer gazer maser phaser praiser
razor stargazer

**Lash** ash balderdash bash brash cash clash crash dash flash
gnash rash rehash slash smash splash stash thrash trash

**Last** aghast blast cast classed contrast fast flabbergast forecast
gassed mast outlast overcast passed past vast

**Late** (see **Ate**)

**Latin** battin' cattin' fatten flatten Manhattan paten Patton

**Latitude** attitude gratitude platitude

**Laugh** calf carafe epitaph giraffe graph paragraph phonograph
photograph polygraph riffraff staff telegraph

**Laughter** after grafter hereafter rafter thereafter

**Lawn**  (see **Dawn**)

**Lazy**  crazy daisy hazy

**Lead**  ahead bed bedspread bread bred coed dead dread fed
    figurehead fled flowerbed fountainhead gingerbread head
    inbred led misled misread overfed read red riverbed said
    shed shred sled sped spread thoroughbred thread
    underfed unthread wed

**Leaf**  beef belief brief chief disbelief grief relief thief

**League**  fatigue intrigue

**Leak**  beak bleak creek eek freak meek reek seek speak
    tweak weak week

**Lean**  (see **Mean**)

**Leap**  barkeep cheep creep deep heap keep peep reap seep
    sheep sleep steep sweep weep

**Learn**  adjourn burn churn concern discern earn fern intern
    kern overturn return sojourn spurn stern taciturn turn
    urn yearn

**Leash**  quiche unleash

**Least**  beast ceased creased deceased east feast pieced
    priest yeast

**Leather**  altogether feather Heather tether together weather
    whether (see *her*)

**Leave**  achieve believe bereave conceive disbelieve eve
    grieve heave perceive receive relieve reprieve retrieve
    sleeve weave

**Lecture**  architecture conjecture

**Ledge**  allege dredge edge fledge hedge privilege sacrilege
    sledge wedge

**Left**  deft theft

**Legal**  beagle eagle illegal regal sea gull

**Leisure**  seizure

**Lend**  (see **Friend**)

**L**

129

**Length**  strength

**Less**  access address baroness bashfulness bitterness bless caress
chess cleverness cloudiness compress confess craziness
deadliness depress digress distress dizziness dress duress
eagerness easiness eeriness emptiness excess express
foolishness ghostliness guess happiness haziness
homelessness idleness impress joyfulness joylessness
laziness limitless Loch Ness lustfulness mess nervousness
obsess openness oppress outrageousness penniless
playfulness possess press profess progress queasiness recess
regress repossess repress rockiness seediness shallowness
silkiness sleaziness sleepiness sneakiness SOS spaciousness
spitefulness stress success suppress thoughtfulness
transgress uselessness viciousness willingness wishfulness
worldliness yes youthfulness

**Let**  (see **Met**)

**Letter**  better debtor getter setter sweater wetter

**Level**  bedevil bevel devil dishevel level revel

**Lewd**  (see **Feud**)

**Liar**  amplifier beautifier briar buyer crier cryer drier dryer
flier friar higher mystifier occupier prior simplifier slyer
supplier testifier (see *fire*)

**Liberty**  (see **Be**)

**Librarian**  (see **Vegetarian**)

**Lick**  arithmetic arsenic brick candlestick candlewick Catholic
chick click flick heartsick hick kick limerick love-sick lunatic
maverick nick pick sick slick stick thick tic tick wick

**Lid**  bid did forbid grid hid invalid kid Madrid pyramid rid
skid slid squid

**Lie**  alibi amplify banzai barfly butterfly buy by bye certify
clarify crucify cry defy deify deny die dignify diversify

**L**

dragonfly drive-by dry dye eye firefly fly fry glorify gratify guy high horrify I identify imply July justify lullaby modify my mystify notify passerby pie pry qualify rely rye satisfy sci-fi shy sigh signify simplify sky sly specify spry spy terrify testify thigh tie try underlie verify why

**Lied**  (see **Bride**)

**Lies**  advertise advise analyze apologize arise authorize baptize capitalize capsize characterize comprise compromise criticize demise deputize despise devise dies disguise economize emphasize enterprise epitomize eulogize excise exercise exorcise eyes familiarize fertilize flies generalize hypnotize idealize idolize immortalize improvise italicize legalize materialize memorize merchandise minimize neutralize ostracize paralyze patronize penalize personalize philosophize plagiarize prize rationalize realize recognize reprise revise rise satirize scandalize scrutinize size socialize specialize spies sterilize stigmatize subsidize summarize sunrise supervise surmise surprise sympathize terrorize theorize thighs ties tranquilize utilize verbalize visualize vocalize wise

**Life**  afterlife jackknife knife strive wife

**Lift**  drift gift shift spendthrift swift thrift

**Light**  appetite bite blight bright byte contrite copyright daylight delight despite dynamite excite Fahrenheit fight flight fright headlight height ignite invite kite knight midnight might moonlight night outright parasite plight polite quite recite reunite right satellite sight site sleight slight spite starlight sunlight tight trite twilight unite white write

**Like**  bike hike mike spike strike tyke

**Liking**  biking disliking spiking striking Viking

**Lily**  Billy Chile Chili chilly dilly filly frilly hillbilly hilly Philly Piccadilly piccalilli shrilly silly willy-nilly

**Limb**  brim dim grim gym hymn pseudonym skim slim swim trim whim

**Limber**  timber timbre

**Lime**  climb crime dime I'm pantomime prime rhyme slime summertime thyme time

**Limp**  blimp gimp pimp shrimp skimp wimp

**Line**  (see **Fine**)

**Lingo**  bingo dingo flamingo gringo jingo (see *glow*)

**Lion**  buyin' cryin' dandelion denyin' dyin' lyin' Orion Ryan sighin' tryin' Zion (see *in*)

**List**  (see **Mist**)

**Listen**  christen dissin' glisten hissin' kissin' missin'

**Live**  affirmative alternative argumentative combative competitive consecutive conservative definitive expletive figurative forgive fugitive give informative intuitive lucrative narrative negative positive primitive prohibitive provocative relative representative sensitive talkative tentative

**Livid**  vivid

**Lizard**  blizzard gizzard scissored wizard

**Load**  (see **Road**)

**Loaf**  oaf

**Loan**  (see **Lone**)

**Lobster**  mobster

**Local**  focal vocal yokel

**Lock**  Bangkok beanstalk boondock clock cock cornstalk crock deadlock defrock dock flintlock flock frock gawk gridlock hawk hock J. S. Bach jock knock Little Rock livestock mock Mohawk padlock peacock rock shock sidewalk small talk smock sock squawk stalk stock talk tomahawk unlock walk wok

**L**

**Locket**  docket hocket pocket rocket socket sprocket (see *it*)

**Lodge**  dislodge dodge hodgepodge lodge

**Loft**  aloft oft soft

**London**  undone (see *done*)

**Lone**  alone atone backbone baritone blown bone chaperone
clone condone cone cornerstone cyclone Dictaphone
flown full-blown full-grown gramophone grindstone
groan grown headstone known loan microphone
milestone moan monotone mown overgrown
overthrown own phone postpone prone saxophone
sewn shown stone telephone thrown tone trombone
unknown xylophone zone

**Loner**  condoner donor groaner honer known 'er loan 'er
loaner moaner owner phone 'er toner

**Long**  along belong bong ding-dong gong Hong Kong
Ping-Pong prong song strong throng wrong

**Longing**  belonging prolonging wronging

**Look**  book brook cook crook hook mistook nook outlook
rook shook took undertook

**Looking**  booking cooking hooking rooking

**Loon**  (see **Moon**)

**Loose**  caboose goose moose noose papoose recluse spruce
truce vamoose

**Lord**  aboard accord afford award board bored ford
harpsichord hoard overboard poured reward shuffleboard
soared sword ward

**Los Angeles**  exodus helluva mess man jealous romances us
scandalous unanimous unscramble us upper crust

**Lose**  blues booze bruise choose cruise news ooze
snooze whose

**Loss**  across albatross boss cross double-cross floss gloss
moss rhinoceros sauce toss

**Lost** bossed cost crossed exhaust flossed frost holocaust
Pentecost tossed

**Lot** (see **Hot**)

**Lottery** pottery watery

**Loud** allowed aloud cloud crowd enshroud plowed proud
shroud thundercloud

**Louder** chowder powder prouder (see *her*)

**Lounge** scrounge

**Love** above dove glove ladylove mourning dove of shove
turtle dove

**Lover** cover discover hover recover rediscover shover
undercover (see *her*)

**Low** (see **Blow**)

**L**

**Loyal** broil coil foil oil recoil royal spoil toil turmoil

**Loyalty** royalty (see *be*)

**Luck** amuck buck chuck cluck deduct duck horror-struck
muck pluck potluck puck struck suck truck tuck

**Lucky** ducky Kentucky unlucky

**Lumber** cucumber cumber encumber number
slumber umber

**Lump** bump chump clump dump hump jump plump rump
slump stump thump trump ump

**Lunar** communer crooner harpooner lampooner pruner
schooner sooner spooner tuner

**Lunch** brunch bunch crunch hunch munch punch scrunch

**Lure** (see **Cure**)

**Lust** adjust August bust crust disgust distrust encrust entrust
gust just mistrust must robust rust thrust trust unjust

**Luxury** (see *be*)

**Lynch** cinch flinch inch pinch

**Lyrical** empirical miracle satirical

# M

**Machine** (see **Mean**)

**Machinery** beanery greenery scenery

**Mad** ad add bad Brad cad Chad clad Dad egad fad glad grad
had lad nomad pad plaid sad shad Trinidad

**Made** afraid aid arcade barricade blade blockade braid brayed
brigade centigrade charade crusade degrade dismayed
dissuade downgrade escapade evade fade grade grenade
hayed invade laid lemonade maid masquerade paid parade
persuade played promenade raid renegade serenade
shade spade stockade suede tirade trade

**Madonna** belladonna Donna iguana prima donna wanna

**Magic** tragic (see *tick*)

**Magician** (see *tradition*)

**Mail** (see **Ale**)

**Main** abstain again airplane arraign ascertain attain brain Cain
campaign cane chain champagne cocaine complain contain
crane detain disdain domain drain entertain explain feign
gain grain humane hurricane hydroplane insane lane
Maine maintain mane migraine obtain ordain pain pane
pertain plain plane profane propane rain refrain reign rein
remain sane slain Spain sprain stain strain sustain train
vain vane vein wane windowpane

**Major** cager pager stager wager

**Make** ache bake brake break cake fake flake forsake headache
heartache keepsake mistake opaque quake rake sake
shake snake stake steak take wake

**Male** (see **Ale**)

**Malevolent** benevolent

**Malice** Alice chalice Dallas palace phallus

**Mall**   all ball bawl brawl call crawl doll drawl fall gall haul install
    maul Montreal nightfall overhaul parasol pitfall protocol
    rainfall scrawl shawl small snowfall sprawl stall tall thrall
    wall waterfall y'all

**Malt**   assault cobalt exalt fault halt salt somersault vault

**Mamma**   Bahama comma Dalai Lama drama llama melodrama
    pajama Yokohama

**Man**   ban can can-can Dan fan Iran Nan plan ran Tehran

**Maneuver**   Hoover mover prover remover Vancouver

**Manic**   (see **Volcanic**)

**Manor**   banner canner fanner manner planner scanner
    spanner tanner

**Manual**   annual

**Many**   any Benny Jenny penny

**Map**   cap chap clap flap gap handicap lap mishap nap rap sap
    scrap slap snap strap tap trap wrap zap

**Maple**   papal staple

**March**   arch parch starch

**Mark**   aardvark arc ark bark dark embark hark lark narc park
    patriarch remark shark spark stark

**Marquee**   malarkey marquis oligarchy patriarchy

**Marriage**   carriage disparage miscarriage

**Marry**   carry hairy hari-kari miscarry parry vary (see *cherry*)

**Marrying**   carrying

**Marsh**   harsh

**Martyr**   barter Carter charter darter garter smarter
    starter tarter

**Mash**   ash balderdash bash brash cash clash crash dash flash
    gnash lash rash rehash slash smash splash stash thrash trash

**Mask**   ask bask cask flask task

**Match**  attach batch catch detach dispatch hatch latch
patch scratch snatch

**Mate**  (see **Ate**)

**Material**  cereal immaterial managerial ministerial serial

**Math**  aftermath bath homeopath path psychopath
sociopath wrath

**Matrimony**  acrimony alimony baloney bony crony
macaroni patrimony phony pony sanctimony stony
testimony Tony

**May**  (see **Say**)

**Maybe**  baby (see *be*)

**Mayor**  betrayer conveyor grayer layer payer player portrayer
prayer slayer soothsayer sprayer stayer surveyor

**Me**  (see **Be**)

**Mean**  bean between caffeine canteen chlorine clean codeine
Colleen convene cuisine dean demean evergreen
Florentine foreseen gasoline Gene green guillotine
Halloween in-between intervene kerosene lean lien
machine marine mezzanine Nazarene nectarine nicotine
obscene preen quarantine queen ravine routine sardine
scene seen serene spleen submarine tambourine
tangerine teen thirteen (etc.) Vaseline velveteen
wintergreen wolverine

**Meant**  (see **Bent**)

**Measure**  displeasure pleasure treasure

**Meat**  (see **Meet**)

**Mechanical**  botanical manacle tyrannical

**Medal**  meddle pedal peddle

**Medium**  tedium (see *some*)

**Meek**  beak bleak creek eek freak leak reek seek speak
tweak weak week

**M**

**Meet** athlete beat beet bittersweet bleat cheat compete
complete conceit concrete deceit defeat delete deplete
discreet discrete eat elite feat feet fleet greet heat
incomplete indiscreet meat meet mistreat neat obsolete
parakeet receipt repeat retreat seat sheet sleet street
suite sweet treat wheat

**Melancholy** collie dolly finale folly golly jolly Molly Polly
tamale trolley volley

**Mellow** bellow cello fellow hello Othello yellow

**Melodic** episodic methodic periodic

**Melody** (see **Be**)

**Melt** belt Celt dealt felt heartfelt pelt welt

**Member** December dismember ember November
remember September

**Memo** demo

**M**

**Memory** (see **Be**)

**Men** amen citizen den fen hen hydrogen Ken oxygen pen
regimen specimen ten then yen zen

**Menace** tennis

**Mend** (see **Friend**)

**Menial** congenial

**Mental** accidental coincidental complemental continental
dental departmental detrimental experimental
fundamental gentle governmental incidental
intercontinental lentil monumental Oriental parental
regimental rental rudimental sentimental
supplemental temperamental

**Mess** access address baroness bashfulness bitterness bless
caress chess cleverness cloudiness compress confess
craziness deadliness depress digress distress dizziness
dress duress eagerness easiness eeriness emptiness
excess express finesse foolishness ghostliness guess

happiness haziness homelessness idleness impress
joyfulness joylessness laziness less limitless Loch
Ness lustfulness nervousness obsess openness oppress
outrageousness penniless playfulness possess press
profess progress queasiness recess regress repossess
repress rockiness seediness shallowness silkiness
sleaziness sleepiness sneakiness SOS spaciousness
spitefulness stress success suppress thoughtfulness
transgress uselessness viciousness willingness wishfulness
worldliness yes youthfulness

**Messiah** Jeremiah Maya papaya

**Messy** dressy

**Met** alphabet bayonet bet brunette cabinet cadet cigarette
clarinet cornet corvette debt duet epithet etiquette
forget fret gazette get jet Joliet Juliet let luncheonette
marionette net omelet pet quartet regret roulette set
silhouette Somerset sunset sweat threat Tibet toilette
upset vet 'vette violet wet yet

**M**

**Metal** kettle mettle petal resettle settle

**Mice** advice concise device dice entice ice lice nice
paradise precise price rice sacrifice spice splice suffice
thrice twice vice

**Middle** diddle fiddle griddle riddle twiddle

**Midget** digit fidget widget

**Might** (see **Night**)

**Mild** child dialed piled smiled wild

**Mile** (see **Smile**)

**Military** (see **Ordinary**)

**Milk** bilk ilk silk

**Million** billion Brazilian Maximillian pavilion reptilian
trillion zillion

**Millionaire** (see **Air**)

**Mind**  behind bind blind find grind hind humankind kind
mastermind remind signed unkind unwind wind wined

**Mine**  align asinine assign benign combine concubine confine
consign decline define design dine divine entwine feline
fine incline line malign nine outshine pine porcupine
recline refine resign Rhine shine shrine sign spine stein
swine twine underline undermine vine whine wine

**Mingle**  intermingle jingle Kris Kringle shingle single tingle

**Miniature**  (see **Pure**)

**Minister**  administer sinister

**Minor**  cosigner designer diner eyeliner finer liner miner
refiner shiner signer

**Mint**  flint hint lint spearmint peppermint print splint sprint
squint tint

**Minus**  sinus (see *us*)

**M**

**Minute**  spinet (see *it*)

**Miracle**  empirical lyrical satirical

**Mirage**  barrage camouflage garage entourage

**Mirror**  cheerer clearer dearer hearer jeerer nearer queerer
severer sneerer spearer

**Misery**  (see **Be**)

**Miss**  abyss amiss analysis armistice bliss carcass cowardice
'diss dismiss emphasis hiss hypothesis kiss nemesis office
prejudice Swiss synthesis this

**Missile**  bristle dismissal gristle missal sisal thistle whistle

**Mission**  (see **Tradition**)

**Mist**  accompanist analyst anarchist anthropologist archeologist
assist biologist Calvinist capitalist coexist communist
consist cyst desist dismissed egoist essayist evangelist
exist exorcist fatalist gist hissed humanist humorist
idealist imperialist insist journalist kissed list lobbyist
Methodist missed moralist motorist nationalist novelist

> organist perfectionist pharmacist pianist plagiarist
> psychologist romanticist satirist sentimentalist socialist
> soloist specialist strategist terrorist theologist theorist
> twist ventriloquist vocalist wrist

**Mistake**   ache bake brake break cake fake flake forsake
> headache heartache keepsake make opaque quake rake
> shake snake stake steak take wake

**Mistaken**   achin' bacon forsaken Jamaican makin' overtaken
> shaken undertaken taken unshaken waken

**Mister**   assister blister magister resister sister
> twister (see *her*)

**Misty**   Christie Corpus Christi twisty (see *tea*)

**Mitt**   befit bit fit 'git grit kit knit hit it lit nit-wit pit quit sit twit
> unfit ultimate wit zit

**Mix**   acrobatics bics crucifix fiddlesticks fix kicks licks
> mathematics nix picks politics six sticks Styx ticks transfix
> tricks wicks

**Mixer**   elixir fixer (see *her*)

**Mixture**   fixture

**Moan**   alone atone backbone baritone blown bone chaperone
> clone condone cone cornerstone cyclone Dictaphone
> flown full-blown full-grown gramophone grindstone groan
> grown headstone known loan lone microphone milestone
> monotone mown overgrown overthrown own phone
> postpone prone saxophone sewn shown stone telephone
> thrown tone trombone unknown xylophone zone

**Mob**   blob bob cob fob gob hob hobnob job knob lob nob
> rob slob snob sob swab throb

**Mobster**   lobster

**Mock**   (see **Shock**)

**Model**   coddle remodel swaddle toddle twaddle waddle

**Mogul**   ogle

**M**

**Moist**  hoist joist rejoiced voiced

**Molester**  Chester contester fester investor jester Lester
pester protester semester sequester tester
Westchester Winchester

**Mom**  aplomb bomb calm embalm Guam palm psalm qualm

**Monday**  one day Sunday (see *day*)

**Money**  bunny funny honey runny sunny

**Monk**  bunk chunk clunk cyberpunk drunk dunk flunk funk hunk
junk plunk punk shrunk skunk slunk spunk stunk sunk trunk

**Monkey**  chunky flunky funky spunky

**Mood**  brood clued conclude crude dude exclude food glued
include intrude misconstrued mood preclude prude rude
seclude shrewd wooed

**Moon**  afternoon baboon balloon bassoon boon buffoon
cartoon cocoon coon croon goon harpoon harvest moon
honeymoon lagoon lampoon loon maroon monsoon
noon platoon prune raccoon saloon Saskatoon soon
spittoon swoon tycoon typhoon (see *tune*)

**Moose**  caboose goose loose noose papoose recluse spruce
truce vamoose

**Mop**  (see **Drop**)

**Moral**  aural choral floral immoral laurel oral

**More**  (see **Door**)

**Mortal**  chortle immortal portal

**Most**  boast coast foremost furthermost ghost host innermost
post roast toast whipping post

**Mother**  another brother other smother

**Motion**  commotion emotion locomotion lotion notion ocean
potion promotion

**Motive**  emotive locomotive

**Motto**  blotto grotto legato staccato

**M**

**Mound** (see **Found**)

**Mountain** countin' fountain

**Mourn** adorn airborne born Cape Horn Capricorn forlorn forsworn horn lovelorn Matterhorn morn popcorn scorn seaborne stillborn sworn unicorn warn worn

**Mouse** blouse douse grouse house louse madhouse outhouse penthouse slaughterhouse souse spouse

**Move** approve behoove disapprove disprove groove improve prove remove

**Movie** groovy

**Mow** (see **Blow**)

**Much** clutch crutch Dutch hutch inasmuch retouch such touch

**Muck** (see **Truck**)

**Mud** blood bud cud dud flood mud scud spud stud thud

**Muffin** puffin ragamuffin stuffin' toughen

**Muffle** duffle ruffle scuffle shuffle truffle

**Mule** molecule ridicule vestibule Yule

**Mumble** bumble crumble fumble grumble humble jumble mumble rumble stumble tumble

**Mural** extramural intramural neural plural rural

**Murder** girder herder

**Muscle** bustle corpuscle hustle mussel rustle tussle

**Music** arsenic brick candlestick Catholic chick click flick heartsick hick kick lick limerick love-sick maverick nick pick sick slick stick thick tic tick

**Musician** (see **Tradition**)

**Muss** (see **Us**)

**Must** adjust August bust crust disgust distrust encrust entrust gust just lust mistrust robust rust thrust trust unjust

**Mustard** custard

**My** (see **Cry**)

**Mystery** history

**M**

# N

**Nail**  (see **Ale**)

**Name**  acclaim aim became blame came claim exclaim
fame flame frame game inflame lame maim proclaim
same shame tame

**Narc**  aardvark arc ark bark dark embark hark lark mark
park patriarch remark shark spark stark

**Narcotic**  chaotic erotic exotic hypnotic idiotic
macrobiotic quixotic

**Narrate**  (see **Ate**)

**Narrow**  arrow barrow harrow marrow sparrow tarot

**National**  international irrational rational passional

**Native**  accumulative appreciative authoritative communicative
creative decorative generative hesitative imitative
innovative investigative operative vindictive

**Naughty**  dotty knotty manicotti spotty

**Near**  adhere appear atmosphere auctioneer beer bombardier
career cashier cavalier chandelier cheer clear dear
deer disappear ear engineer fear financier frontier gear
hear hemisphere here insincere interfere jeer lavaliere
leer mere mountaineer overhear overseer peer persevere
pioneer queer racketeer reappear rear revere seer severe
shear sheer sincere smear sneer spear sphere
stratosphere tear veneer volunteer year

**Neat**  (see **Meet**)

**Necessary**  (see **Ordinary**)

**Neck**  check Czech deck fleck heck peck Quebec speck
trek wreck

**Need**  agreed breed centipede concede creed deed exceed
feed greed heed inbreed knead lead mislead precede
proceed read recede reed secede seed speed stampede
succeed Swede tweed weed

**Neglect**  (see **Effect**)

**Neighbor**  belabor labor saber

**Neither**  breather either

**Neon**  eon peon (see *dawn*)

**Nerve**  conserve curve deserve observe preserve reserve
serve swerve

**Nest**  (see **Best**)

**Never**  clever endeavor ever forever however lever sever
whatever whenever wherever whoever

**New**  adieu anew avenue barbecue bayou chew choo-choo
cue curfew debut dew due ensue ewe few guru
honeydew hue I.O.U. imbue ingénue interview Jew knew
ieu new Nehru overdue pee-ewe pew preview pursue
renew residue revenue review spew subdue sue undue
view yew you (see *do*)

**New York**  cork fork pitchfork pork stork torque uncork

**Next**  context flexed pretext text

**Nibble**  dribble kibble quibble scribble Sibyl

**Nice**  advice concise device dice entice ice lice mice
paradise precise price rice sacrifice spice splice suffice
thrice twice vice

**Night**  appetite bite blight bright byte contrite copyright
daylight delight despite dynamite excite Fahrenheit
fight flight fright headlight height ignite invite kite knight
light midnight might moonlight outright parasite plight
polite quite recite reunite right satellite sight site sleight
slight spite starlight sunlight tight trite twilight unite
white write

**N**

**Nightmare** (see **Air**)

**Nile** (see **Smile**)

**Nirvana** Americana banana bandanna Diana Hannah Havana hosanna Indiana Louisiana Pollyanna Savannah Texarkana

**No** afro although banjo beau below bestow blow bow buffalo bungalow calico crossbow crow depot doe domino dough embryo escrow Eskimo flow foe forgo fro gazebo gigolo glow go grow heigh-ho ho-ho hobo hoe incognito indigo Joe know long ago low Mexico mistletoe mow oboe oh outgrow overflow overgrow overthrow owe Pinocchio pistachio plateau quo rainbow ratio roe row sew slow snow so Soho status quo stow studio tally-ho though throw tiptoe to-and-fro toe Tokyo tow tremolo undergo undertow vertigo woe yo yo-yo

**Nobody** body embody gaudy lawdy shoddy somebody toddy

**Nocturnal** colonel eternal external fraternal infernal internal journal kernel maternal paternal

**Nod** abroad applaud awed broad clod cod defraud façade fraud God guffawed Izod odd pod prod promenade quad rod roughshod shod sod squad trod wad

**Noise** poise

**None** anyone begun bun comparison done everyone fun Galveston gun hon Hun jettison nun oblivion one outdone outrun overdone overrun phenomenon pun run shun simpleton skeleton son stun sun ton unison venison won

**Noodle** boodle caboodle doodle feudal poodle Yankee Doodle

**Noon** afternoon baboon balloon bassoon boon buffoon cartoon cocoon coon croon goon harpoon harvest moon honeymoon lagoon lampoon loon maroon monsoon

**N**

moon platoon prune raccoon saloon Saskatoon soon
spittoon swoon tycoon typhoon (see *tune*)

**Noose**  caboose goose loose moose papoose recluse spruce
truce vamoose

**Normal**  abnormal formal informal

**North**  forth fourth henceforth

**Not**  apricot blot Camelot clot cot cybot dot forget-me-not
forgot fought gavotte got hot hot-shot jot knot lot plot
pot robot rot shot slingshot somewhat spot squat swat
tot trot watt what yacht

**Notate**  rotate (see *ate*)

**Notch**  blotch botch crotch debauch hopscotch
Scotch wristwatch

**Note**  afloat antidote bloat boat coat connote denote dote
float footnote gloat goat misquote moat oat overcoat
promote quote remote riverboat rote smote throat tote
underwrote vote wrote

**Notorious**  (see **Us**)

**Novel**  grovel hovel

**Now**  allow avow bough bow brow chow cow disavow endow
frau how kowtow ow plough plow row slough somehow
sow thou vow wow

**Nude**  (see **Feud**)

**Numb**  album aquarium auditorium become bum burdensome
Christendom come cranium crematorium crumb
curriculum dumb drum emporium fee-fi-fo-fum glum gum
gymnasium hum kettledrum kingdom martyrdom maximum
meddlesome medium millennium minimum mum museum
opium overcome pendulum petroleum platinum plum
premium quarrelsome radium random rum sanitarium scum
slum some strum succumb sum swum tedium thumb Tom
Thumb Tweedledum uranium worrisome yum

**Number**   cucumber cumber encumber lumber
        slumber umber

**Nurse**   adverse converse curse disburse disperse diverse
        hearse immerse intersperse inverse purse rehearse
        reverse terse transverse traverse universe verse worse

**Nursery**   anniversary cursory

**Nurture**   searcher

**Nutty**   putty smutty

N

# O

**Oaf** loaf

**Oath** both growth loath overgrowth undergrowth

**Obey** (see **Say**)

**Object** (see **Defect**)

**Objection** (see **Rejection**)

**Obscenity** amenity identity serenity

**Observe** conserve curve deserve nerve preserve reserve
serve swerve

**Occasion** abrasion dissuasion equation evasion
invasion persuasion

**Ocean** commotion emotion locomotion lotion motion
notion potion promotion

**Odd** abroad applaud awed broad clod cod defraud façade
fraud God guffawed Izod nod pod prod promenade quad
rod roughshod shod sod squad trod wad

**Ode** (see **Road**)

**Odor** exploder goader loader

**Of** above dove glove ladylove love mourning dove shove
turtle dove

**Off** cough scoff trough

**Offensive** apprehensive comprehensive defensive expensive
extensive incomprehensive inexpensive intensive pensive

**Offer** coffer cougher scoffer

**Often** coffin coughin' soften

**Office** abyss amiss analysis armistice bliss carcass cowardice
'diss dismiss emphasis hiss hypothesis kiss miss nemesis
prejudice Swiss synthesis this

**Ogle** mogul

**Oh** (see **So**)

**Oil** broil coil foil loyal recoil royal spoil toil turmoil

149

**Old**  behold blindfold bold centerfold cold fold foothold
foretold gold hold household marigold mold retold scold
sold told uphold withhold

**On**  Amazon autobahn Babylon bonbon Bonn brawn chiffon
con dawn drawn echelon fawn gone lawn neon pawn
pentagon silicon swan undergone upon wan woebegone
wonton yawn

**Once**  bunts dunce fronts

**One**  anyone begun bun comparison done everyone fun
Galveston gun hon Hun jettison none nun oblivion
outdone outrun overdone overrun phenomenon pun
run shun simpleton skeleton son stun sun ton unison
venison won

**Only**  lonely

**Ooze**  blues booze bruise choose cruise lose news ooze
snooze whose

**Opt**  adopt copped flopped mopped popped stopped

**Or**  (see **Door**)

**Orchard**  tortured

**Order**  boarder border disorder hoarder recorder

**Ordinary**  adversary airy arbitrary beneficiary berry bury
canary capillary cautionary cherry commentary culinary
customary dairy dictionary dietary dignitary disciplinary
discretionary evolutionary extraordinary fairy February
ferry functionary hairy hereditary honorary imaginary
incendiary intermediary January Jerry legendary legionary
literary luminary Mary mercenary military momentary
monetary mortuary nary necessary obituary Perry
planetary prairie proprietary pulmonary reactionary
revolutionary sanctuary sanitary scary secretary seminary
sherry solitary stationary temporary Terry Tipperary very
visionary vocabulary voluntary wary

**Organ**  gorgon Morgan

**Other**  another brother mother smother

**Ouch**  couch crouch grouch pouch slouch vouch

**Ounce**  announce bounce counts denounce mounts pounce
        pronounce renounce trounce

**Our**  devour flour hour scour (see *flower*)

**Out**  about boy scout blow-out bout clout devout doubt eke
        out flout gout lout pout roundabout route scout shout
        snout spout sprout stout tout trout wash-out worn-out

**Outsider**  chider cider decider divider glider insider low-rider
        provider rider slider spider wider

**Oven**  lovin' shovin' sloven

**Over**  clover Dover drover moreover rover

**Overload**  a la mode abode bode code corrode episode
        erode explode forebode goad load lode mode mowed
        lode ode road rode sowed toad unload

**Overwhelm**  elm helm realm whelm

**Owe**  (see **Blow**)

**O**

**Owl**  cowl foul fowl growl howl jowl prowl scowl waterfowl

**Own**  alone atone backbone baritone blown bone chaperone
        clone condone cone cornerstone cyclone Dictaphone
        flown full-blown full-grown gramophone grindstone groan
        grown headstone known loan lone microphone milestone
        moan monotone mown overgrown overthrown phone
        postpone prone saxophone sewn shown stone telephone
        thrown tone trombone unknown xylophone zone

**Owner**  condoner donor groaner honer known 'er loan 'er
        loaner loner moaner owner phone 'er toner

**Ox**  box chickenpox equinox fox mailbox orthodox paradox

**Oxygen**  amen citizen den fen hen hydrogen men Ken pen
        regimen specimen ten then yen zen

# P

**Pacific**  hieroglyphic horrific prolific scientific specific terrific

**Pack**  almanac attack back black bric-a-brac Cadillac cardiac
clickety-clack egomaniac feedback hack Hackensack
haystack jack kleptomaniac knack lack maniac plaque
Pontiac prozac quack rack sack shack slack snack stack
tack track whack yak zodiac

**Packet**  bracket jacket racket (see *it*)

**Packing**  backing cracking hacking lacking ransacking smacking
tracking whacking

**Paddle**  saddle straddle

**Page**  age cage gage rampage sage stage wage

**Paid**  aid arcade afraid barricade blade blockade braid brayed
brigade centigrade charade crusade degrade dismayed
dissuade downgrade escapade evade fade grade grenade
hayed invade laid lemonade made maid masquerade
parade persuade played promenade raid renegade
serenade shade spade stockade suede tirade trade

**Pain**  abstain again airplane arraign ascertain attain brain Cain
campaign cane chain champagne cocaine complain contain
crane detain disdain domain drain entertain explain feign
gain grain humane hurricane hydroplane insane lane main
Maine maintain mane migraine obtain ordain pane pertain
plain plane profane propane rain refrain reign rein remain
sane slain Spain sprain stain strain sustain train vain vane
vein wane windowpane

**Paint**  acquaint ain't complaint faint quaint restraint saint
taint 'tain't

**Pair**  (see **Air**)

**Pal**  canal chorale gal morale shall

**Palace**  Alice chalice Dallas malice phallus

**Panel**  channel flannel

**Panic**  (see **Volcanic**)

**Paper**  caper draper escaper scraper shaper skyscraper
taper (see *her*)

**Parachute**  (see **Shoot**)

**Parade**  (see **Afraid**)

**Paradise**  advice concise device dice entice ice lice mice
nice precise price rice sacrifice spice splice suffice thrice
twice vice

**Parent**  apparent grandparent transparent (see *ant*)

**Park**  aardvark arc ark bark dark embark hark lark mark narc
patriarch remark shark spark stark

**Parody**  (see **Be**)

**Parole**  (see **Roll**)

**Parrot**  carat carrot ferret merit tear it wear it (see *sit*)

**Parted**  broken-hearted carted charted chicken-hearted cold-
hearted darted departed fainthearted halfhearted
hardhearted lion-hearted smarted started

**Particle**  article nautical

**Party**  arty hearty smarty tarty

**Pass**  (see **Class**)

**Passion**  ashen bashin' compassion fashion impassion

**Past**  aghast blast cast classed contrast fast flabbergast
forecast gassed last mast outlast overcast passed vast

**Pastor**  blaster caster castor disaster faster flabbergaster
forecaster master plaster postmaster taskmaster

**Patch**  attach batch catch detach dispatch hatch latch match
scratch snatch

**Path**  aftermath bath homeopath math psychopath
sociopath wrath

**P**

**Pathetic**  aesthetic alphabetic apathetic apologetic arithmetic athletic cosmetic electromagnetic energetic frenetic genetic poetic sympathetic synthetic theoretic

**Patrol**  (see **Roll**)

**Pauper**  (see **Proper**)

**Pause**  applause because cause clause claws gauze laws menopause Oz paws Santa Claus was

**Pawn**  Amazon Babylon begone bonbon Bonn brawn chiffon con Don dawn drawn fawn gone hexagon John lawn lexicon octagon on Oregon pentagon silicon undergone upon withdrawn wanton yawn

**Pay**  array bay betray bluejay bouquet bray clay day decay delay disarray dismay display eh? essay exposé fray gay gray hay hey holiday hooray José Kay lay matinee may moiré naysay negligée obey play portray protégé ray résumé ricochet risqué rosé say slay sleigh soufflé stay stray sway they toupee way weigh x-ray

**Peace**  cease crease decease decrease fleece geese grease Greece increase lease mantelpiece masterpiece piece police release

**Pearl**  curl earl girl hurl swirl twirl whirl

**Pearly**  burly curly girlie squirrelly surly swirly

**Peck**  check Czech deck fleck heck neck Quebec speck trek wreck

**Pedal**  medal meddle peddle

**Peep**  barkeep cheep creep deep heap keep leap reap seep sheep sleep steep sweep weep

**Pen**  amen citizen den fen hen hydrogen Ken men oxygen regimen specimen ten then yen zen

**Pencil**  prehensile stencil utensil

**Penny**  any Benny Jenny many

**P**

**People**  Steeple (see *pull*)

**Perfect**  (see **Defect**)

**Perfume**  assume consume costume exhume presume
      resume  (see *room*)

**Perish**  bearish cherish

**Perjury**  surgery

**Perky**  Albuquerque murky quirky turkey

**Permission**  (see **Tradition**)

**Persistent**  assistant consistent distant existent inconsistent
      insistent resistant subsistent

**Persuasive**  dissuasive evasive invasive pervasive

**Pervert**  (see **Hurt**)

**Pest**  (see **Best**)

**Pet**  alphabet bayonet bet brunette cabinet cadet cigarette
      clarinet cornet corvette debt duet forget fret gazette get
      jet Joliet Juliet let luncheonette marionette met net
      omelet pet quartet regret roulette set silhouette
      Somerset sunset sweat threat Tibet toilette upset vet
      'vette violet wet yet

**Petty**  confetti jetty machete spaghetti sweaty

**Phone**  alone atone backbone baritone blown bone
      chaperone clone condone cone cornerstone cyclone
      Dictaphone flown full-blown full-grown gramophone
      grindstone groan grown headstone known loan lone
      microphone milestone moan monotone mown
      overgrown overthrown own phone postpone prone
      saxophone sewn shown stone telephone thrown tone
      trombone unknown xylophone zone

**Phony**  acrimony alimony baloney bony crony
      macaroni matrimony patrimony pony sanctimony
      stony testimony Tony

**P**

**Photo**  De Soto koto roto Toto

**Pianist**  (see **Mist**)

**Pick**  arithmetic arsenic brick candlestick candlewick Catholic
chick click flick heartsick hick kick lick limerick love-sick
lunatic maverick music nick sick slick stick thick tic
tick wick

**Picket**  cricket thicket ticket wicket (see *it*)

**Pie**  (see **Cry**)

**Piece**  cease crease decease decrease fleece geese grease
Greece increase lease mantelpiece masterpiece peace
police release

**Pierce**  fierce

**Pig**  big dig fig gig jig renege rig swig thingamajig twig wig

**Pigeon**  religion widgeon

**Pile**  (see **Smile**)

**Pillage**  tillage village

**Pillar**  caterpillar chiller distiller driller filler instiller killer
shriller spiller swiller thriller tiller

**Pillow**  armadillo billow peccadillo willow

**Pimp**  blimp gimp limp shrimp skimp wimp

**Pimple**  dimple simple

**Pin**  (see **Been**)

**Pinch**  cinch flinch inch lynch

**Pink**  blink brink chink clink drink fink ink kink link mink rink
shrink sink slink stink wink zinc

**Pipe**  archetype gripe hype prototype ripe stereotype stripe
swipe type wipe

**Pistol**  crystal

**Pitied**  prettied

**Pity**  city committee ditty gritty kitty pretty self-pity witty

**Pivot**  divot (see *it*)

**Place**  ace  base bass brace case chase commonplace debase
disgrace displace embrace encase erase face grace lace
mace misplace pace race replace space steeplechase
trace unlace vase

**Plague**  vague

**Plan**  an ban can can-can Dan fan Iran man Nan ran Tehran

**Plane**  (see **Pain**)

**Planet**  gannet granite Janet pomegranate (see *it*)

**Plant**  ant aunt can't chant decant enchant grant implant rant
scant shan't slant transplant

**Plastic**  bombastic drastic elastic enthusiastic fantastic
gymnastic iconoclastic sarcastic scholastic spastic

**Plate**  (see **Ate**)

**Play**  (see **Say**)

**Played**  (see **Afraid**)

**Player**  betrayer conveyor grayer layer mayor payer portrayer
prayer slayer soothsayer sprayer stayer surveyor

**Pleasant**  omnipresent peasant pheasant present

**Pleasure**  displeasure measure treasure

**Plenty**  twenty

**Plot**  (see **Hot**)

**Plummet**  summit (see *it*)

**Plump**  bump chump clump dump hump jump lump rump
slump stump thump trump ump

**Plunge**  lunge sponge

**Plus**  (see **Us**)

**Poem**  chrome chromosome comb dome foam gnome home
honeycomb metronome Nome roam Rome tome

**Poetic**  aesthetic alphabetic apathetic apologetic arithmetic
athletic cosmetic electromagnetic energetic frenetic
genetic pathetic sympathetic synthetic theoretic

**P**

**Point** anoint appoint counterpoint disappoint disjoint joint

**Pole** (see **Roll**)

**Police** cease crease decease decrease fleece geese grease
Greece increase lease mantelpiece masterpiece peace
piece release

**Polish** (See **Abolish**)

**Politician** (see **Tradition**)

**Pollution** (see **Revolution**)

**Pond** beyond blond bond correspond fond dawned respond
spawned vagabond wand yawned

**Ponder** condor conned 'er fonder launder squander
wander yonder

**Pony** acrimony alimony baloney bony crony macaroni
matrimony patrimony phony sanctimony stony
testimony Tony

**Pooch** hooch mooch smooch

**Poodle** boodle caboodle doodle feudal noodle Yankee Doodle

**Pool** April fool cool drool fool ghoul Liverpool overrule rule
school spool stool tool whirlpool

**P**

**Poor** amour boor contour detour moor paramour spoor
tour (see *door*)

**Pop** (see **Drop**)

**Pope** (see **Hope**)

**Porch** scorch torch

**Portion** abortion contortion distortion extortion proportion

**Posh** (see **Wash**)

**Post** boast coast foremost furthermost ghost host innermost
most roast toast whipping post

**Pot**  apricot blot Camelot clot cot cybot dot forget-me-not
forgot fought gavotte got hot hot-shot jot knot lot not
plot robot rot shot slingshot somewhat spot squat swat
tot trot watt what yacht

**Potion**  commotion emotion locomotion lotion motion
notion ocean promotion

**Pound**  (see **Sound**)

**Pour**  (see **Door**)

**Powder**  chowder louder prouder (see *her*)

**Power**  cauliflower cower deflower empower flower
horsepower plower shower tower (see *our*)

**Practical**  didactical tactical

**Prairie**  (see **Ordinary**)

**Prank**  bank blank clank crank dank drank flank frank
hank outrank plank rank sank shrank spank stank
tank thank yank

**Prayer**  (see **Air**)

**Prayer**  betrayer conveyor grayer layer mayor payer player
portrayer slayer soothsayer sprayer stayer surveyor

**Preach**  beach breach each impeach leech peach reach
screech speech teach

**Preacher**  bleacher creature feature screecher teacher

**Precocious**  atrocious ferocious

**Present**  omnipresent peasant pheasant pleasant

**President**  resident (see *bent*)

**Pressure**  fresher refresher thresher (see *sure*)

**Pretender**  (see **Tender**)

**Pretentious**  conscientious contentious

**Pretty**  city committee ditty gritty kitty pity self-pity witty

**P**

**Price** advice concise device dice entice ice lice mice nice
paradise precise rice sacrifice spice splice suffice thrice
twice vice

**Pride** beside bonafide bride collide confide countryside
decide defied died dignified divide eyed fireside guide
hide hillside homicide inside lied outside override
provide reside ride side slide snide stride subdivide
subside suicide tide tried wide yuletide

**Priest** beast ceased creased deceased east feast least
pieced yeast

**Primate** climate (see _it_, _ate_)

**Prime** climb crime dime I'm lime pantomime rhyme slime
summertime thyme time

**Prince** convince hints mints rinse since wince

**Print** flint hint lint mint peppermint spearmint splint
sprint squint tint

**Prior** amplifier beautifier briar buyer crier cryer drier
dryer flier friar higher mystifier occupier simplifier slyer
supplier testifier (see _fire_)

**Prison** arisen risen wizen (see _in_)

**Privilege** allege dredge edge fledge hedge ledge privilege
sacrilege sledge wedge

**Prize** (see **Lies**)

**Probe** disrobe globe Job robe strobe

**Produce** (see **Use**)

**Producer** reducer seducer transducer (see _sir_)

**Profit** prophet (see _it_)

**Progressive** aggressive depressive digressive excessive
expressive impressive possessive regressive successive

**Pronounce** announce bounce counts denounce mounts
ounce pounce renounce trounce

**P**

**Proof**  aloof bulletproof goof hoof roof spoof waterproof
weatherproof

**Proper**  bebopper bopper chopper copper cropper dropper
eavesdropper eyedropper grasshopper hopper improper
pauper popper sharecropper shopper stopper swapper
teenybopper topper whopper (see *her*)

**Prophet**  profit (see *it*)

**Prostitution**  (see **Revolution**)

**Protect**  (see **Defect**)

**Protester**  Chester contester fester investor jester
Lester molester pester semester sequester tester
Westchester Winchester

**Proud**  allowed aloud cloud crowd enshroud loud plowed
shroud thundercloud

**Prove**  approve behoove disapprove disprove groove
improve move remove

**Provoke**  (see **Joke**)

**Prude**  brood clued conclude crude dude exclude food glued
include intrude misconstrued mood preclude rude
seclude shrewd wooed

**Psalm**  aplomb bomb calm embalm Guam Mom palm qualm

**Psychosis**  diagnosis narcosis neurosis prognosis psychosis

**Pub**  Beelzebub bub club cub grub hub hubbub rub rub-a-dub-
dub scrub shrub snub stub sub tub

**Pucker**  bucker chucker clucker sapsucker seersucker
sucker trucker (see *her*)

**Puddle**  cuddle fuddle huddle muddle

**Puke**  duke juke uke

**Pull**  bull cock-and-bull do-able full wool (see *beautiful*)

**Pulse**  convulse impulse repulse

**Pumpkin**  bumpkin

**P**

**Punch**  brunch bunch crunch hunch lunch munch scrunch

**Puncture**  acupuncture conjuncture juncture

**Punk**  bunk chunk clunk cyberpunk drunk dunk flunk funk
　　　　hunk junk monk plunk shrunk skunk slunk spunk stunk
　　　　sunk trunk

**Punt**  affront blunt brunt bunt confront forefront front grunt
　　　　hunt runt shunt stunt

**Pup**  buttercup cup fed up hard-up pick-up pup suckup sup up

**Pupil**  scruple

**Puppy**  guppy yuppie

**Pure**  allure armature assure brochure caricature cocksure
　　　　cure demure endure ensure expenditure forfeiture
　　　　immature impure insecure insure liqueur literature
　　　　lure manicure mature miniature obscure overture
　　　　pedicure premature reassure secure signature sure
　　　　tablature temperature your

**Purge**  (see **Verge**)

**Push**  bush cush

**Put**  afoot foot leadfoot pussyfoot tenderfoot

**Puzzler**  guzzler muzzler

**P**

# Q

**Quaint**  acquaint ain't complaint faint paint restraint saint taint 'tain't

**Quake**  ache bake brake break cake fake flake forsake headache heartache keepsake make mistake opaque rake shake snake stake steak take wake

**Quality**  (see **Be**)

**Qualm**  aplomb bomb calm embalm Guam Mom palm psalm

**Quart**  abort assort cavort comfort contort court davenport deport distort escort exhort export extort fort import passport port report resort retort short snort sort sport support thwart tort transport wart

**Queen**  bean between caffeine canteen chlorine clean codeine Colleen convene cuisine dean demean evergreen Florentine foreseen gasoline Gene green guillotine Halloween in-between intervene kerosene lean lien machine marine mean mezzanine Nazarene nectarine nicotine obscene preen quarantine ravine routine sardine scene seen serene spleen submarine tambourine tangerine teen thirteen (etc.) Vaseline velveteen wintergreen wolverine

**Queer**  (see **Near**)

**Quench**  bench clench drench French monkey wrench stench trench wench wrench

**Quest**  arrest attest best breast chest congest crest detest digest divest double-breast infest ingest interest invest jest manifest molest nest protest request rest single-breast suggest test vest

**Quibble**  dribble kibble nibble scribble sibyl

**Quicken**  chicken sicken stricken thicken (see *in*)

Q

**Quickly**  prickly sickly slickly stickly thickly

**Quiet**  diet riot (see _it_)

**Quip**  battleship chip clip dip drip equip flip grip gyp hip lip nip
rip scrip ship slip snip strip tip trip whip zip

**Quirk**  clerk handiwork irk jerk Kirk lurk murk overwork
perk quirk smirk Turk work

**Quirky**  Albuquerque murky perky turkey

**Quit**  befit bit fit 'git grit kit knit hit it lit mitt nit-wit pit sit
twit unfit ultimate wit zit

**Quite**  appetite bite blight bright byte contrite copyright
daylight delight despite dynamite excite Fahrenheit
fight flight fright headlight height ignite invite kite knight
light midnight might moonlight night outright parasite
plight polite recite reunite right satellite sight site sleight
slight spite starlight sunlight tight trite twilight unite
white write

**Quitter**  counterfeiter critter fitter fritter glitter litter sitter
transmitter twitter (see _her_)

**Quiz**  biz fizz friz his is showbiz 'tis whiz

**Quota**  Dakota iota Minnesota

**Quote**  afloat antidote bloat boat coat connote denote dote
float footnote gloat goat misquote moat note oat
overcoat promote remote riverboat rote smote throat
tote underwrote vote wrote

# R

**Rabble**  babble dabble scrabble

**Racial**  facial glacial spatial

**Racket**  bracket jacket packet (see *it*)

**Rag**  bag brag drag flag gag hag lag mag nag sag shag slag snag
stag swag tag wag

**Raging**  aging caging gauging paging staging waging

**Raid**  (see **Afraid**)

**Rail**  (see **Ale**)

**Rain**  abstain again airplane arraign ascertain attain brain Cain
campaign cane chain champagne cocaine complain contain
crane detain disdain domain drain entertain explain feign
gain grain humane hurricane hydroplane insane lane main
Maine maintain mane migraine obtain ordain pain pane
pertain plain plane profane propane refrain reign rein
remain sane slain Spain sprain stain strain sustain train
vain vane vein wane windowpane

**Rainbow**  (see **Blow**)

**Raindrop**  chop cop crop drop eavesdrop flop hop lollipop
mop plop pop prop shop stop swap tip-top whop

**Rainy**  brainy grainy zany

**Ramble**  amble gamble scramble shamble

**Ran**  an ban can can-can Dan fan Iran Koran man Nan
plan Tehran

**Ranch**  avalanche branch

**Range**  arrange change derange estrange exchange strange

**Rank**  bank blank clank crank dank drank flank frank
Hank outrank plank prank sank shrank spank stank tank
thank yank

**Rant**  (see **Ant**)

**Rap**  cap chap clap flap gap handicap lap map mishap nap sap scrap slap snap strap tap trap wrap zap

**Rapper**  capper clapper dapper flapper handicapper slapper snapper tapper whippersnapper wiretapper wrapper yapper

**Rapture**  capture recapture (see *your*)

**Rare**  (see **Air**)

**Rate**  (see **Ate**)

**Rational**  international irrational national passional

**Rattle**  battle cattle chattel embattle prattle Seattle tattle

**Ravage**  lavage savage scavage

**Raw**  Arkansas awe bra caw claw draw flaw gnaw guffaw hurrah jaw law Ma macaw nah overdraw Pa paw saw seesaw shah slaw squaw straw thaw withdraw

**Razor**  appraiser blazer gazer laser maser phaser praiser stargazer

**Reach**  beach breach each impeach leech peach preach screech speech teach

**React**  (see **Act**)

**Reaction**  (see **Action**)

**R**

**Read**  agreed breed centipede concede creed deed exceed feed greed heed inbreed knead lead mislead need precede proceed recede secede seed speed stampede succeed Swede tweed weed

**Read**  ahead bed bedspread bread bred coed dead dread fed figurehead fled flowerbed fountainhead gingerbread head inbred lead led misled misread overfed red riverbed said shed shred sled sped spread thoroughbred thread underfed unthread wed

**Realm**  elm helm overwhelm whelm

**Rear**  (see **Near**)

**Reason**  pleasin' season sneezin' squeezin' teasin'
      wheezin' (see *son*)

**Receipt**  (see **Meet**)

**Receive**  achieve believe bereave conceive disbelieve eve
      grieve heave leave receive relieve reprieve retrieve
      sleeve weave

**Recent**  decent indecent

**Recital**  entitle title vital

**Recognition**  (see **Tradition**)

**Red**  (see **Said**)

**Redemption**  exemption preemption

**Refinery**  binary finery

**Reflection**  (see **Rejection**)

**Reflex**  complex decks duplex ex flex necks pecks Rolidex
      sex specs Tex unisex

**Region**  collegian Norwegian

**Regret**  alphabet bayonet bet brunette cabinet cadet cigarette
      clarinet cornet corvette debt duet epithet etiquette
      forget fret gazette get jet Joliet Juliet let luncheonette
      marionette met net omelet pet quartet roulette set
      silhouette Somerset sunset sweat threat Tibet toilette
      upset vet 'vette violet wet yet

**R**

**Reject**  (see **Defect**)

**Rejection**  affection bisection circumspection collection
      complexion connection correction defection deflection
      detection direction disaffection dissection ejection
      election erection imperfection infection inflection
      inspection intersection introspection objection perfection
      projection protection reflection resurrection
      retrospection section selection vivisection

**Relax** ax backs fax jacks lax max packs Saks sax slacks
tax wax

**Release** cease crease decease decrease fleece geese
grease Greece increase lease mantelpiece masterpiece
peace piece police

**Reliance** alliance appliance compliance defiance reliance

**Religion** pigeon widgeon

**Religious** litigious prodigious sacrilegious

**Remain** (see **Rain**)

**Remark** aardvark arc ark bark dark embark hark lark mark
narc park patriarch shark spark stark

**Remember** December dismember ember member
November September

**Reminiscing** dismissing 'dissing hissing kissing missing

**Remorse** coarse course divorce endorse force horse
Norse reinforce resource source

**Remove** approve behoove disapprove disprove groove
improve move prove

**Reno** andantino bambino Filipino keno

**Rent** (see **Bent**)

**Rental** accidental coincidental complemental
compliment continental dental departmental
detrimental experimental fundamental gental
governmental incidental intercontinental lentil
mental monumental Oriental parental regimental
rudimental sentimental supplemental temperamental

**Repair** (see **Air**)

**Repeat** (see **Meet**)

**Resemble** assemble dissemble tremble (see *bull*)

**Resident** president (see *bent*)

**Resisted** assisted cysted enlisted existed fisted insisted
listed misted persisted subsisted twisted

**R**

**Respect**  (see **Defect**)

**Rest**  arrest attest best blessed breast Bucharest Budapest celeste chest congest contest crest detest digest divest dressed guessed guest infest ingest interest invest jest manifest messed molest nest pest protest request second-best suggest test unrest vest zest

**Result**  adult catapult consult cult difficult exult insult occult

**Retire**  (see **Fire**)

**Return**  adjourn burn churn concern discern earn fern intern kern learn overturn sojourn spurn stern taciturn turn urn yearn

**Reveal**  (see **Steal**)

**Revenge**  avenge Stonehenge

**Revolt**  bolt colt dolt jolt thunderbolt

**Revolution**  absolution attribution constitution contribution destitution dilution dissolution distribution electrocution evolution execution institution pollution prosecution prostitution resolution retribution solution substitution

**Revolve**  absolve devolve dissolve evolve involve solve

**Revolver**  solver

**Reward**  aboard accord afford award board bored ford harpsichord hoard lord overboard poured shuffleboard soared sword ward

**Rhyme**  chime climb crime dime I'm lime mime pantomime prime slime summertime thyme time

**Rib**  ad lib crib fib glib rib

**Rich**  bewitch bitch ditch enrich glitch hitch pitch snitch stitch switch twitch which

**Rid**  bid did forbid grid hid invalid lid Madrid pyramid skid slid squid

**Riddle**  diddle fiddle griddle middle twiddle

**R**

**Ride**  beside bonafide bride collide confide countryside decide
defied died dignified divide eyed fireside guide hide hillside
homicide inside lied outside override pride provide reside
ride side slide snide stride subdivide subside suicide tide
tried wide yuletide

**Ridge**  abridge bridge fridge

**Ridicule**  molecule mule ridicule vestibule Yule

**Rifle**  Eiffel eyeful rifle stifle trifle

**Rigid**  frigid

**Ring**  anything bring cling ding evening everything fling king
sing sling spring sting string swing thing wing wring (add
"ing" to "action" words, i.e., run(ning), etc.)

**Riot**  diet quiet (see *it*)

**Rip**  (see **Trip**)

**Ripe**  archetype gripe hype pipe prototype stereotype stripe
swipe type wipe

**Ripple**  cripple nipple triple

**Rise**  (see **Lies**)

**Risen**  arisen prison risen wizen (see *in*)

**Rising**  advertising advising agonizing analyzing apologizing
appetizing baptizing compromising criticizing despising
devising disguising equalizing eulogizing evangelizing
exercising generalizing harmonizing improvising
jeopardizing memorizing mesmerizing minimizing
modernizing organizing patronizing plagiarizing
prizing realizing recognizing revising scrutinizing
sizing sterilizing subsidizing supervising surmising
surprising sympathizing tantalizing terrorizing uprising
utilizing visualizing vocalizing

**Risk**  asterisk brisk disk frisk whisk

**Risky**  frisky whiskey

R

**Rival**  arrival revival survival

**River**  deliver giver liver quiver shiver sliver (see *her*)

**Roach**  approach broach coach cockroach encroach
poach reproach

**Road**  a la mode abode bode code corrode episode
erode explode forebode goad load lode mode mowed
lode ode overload rode sowed toad unload

**Roam**  chrome chromosome comb dome foam gnome home
honeycomb metronome Nome poem Rome tome

**Rob**  blob bob cob fob gob hob hobnob job knob lob mob
nob slob snob sob swab throb

**Robber**  clobber dauber jobber slobber swabber

**Robe**  disrobe globe Job probe strobe

**Robust**  (see **Trust**)

**Rock**  Bangkok beanstalk boondock clock cock cornstalk
crock deadlock defrock dock flintlock flock frock gawk
gridlock hawk hock J. S. Bach jock knock Little Rock
livestock lock mock Mohawk padlock peacock shock
sidewalk small talk smock sock squawk stalk stock talk
tomahawk unlock walk wok

**Rocker**  balker blocker Knickerbocker knocker locker mocker
shocker soccer stalker talker walker (see *her*)

**Rocket**  docket hocket locket pocket socket sprocket (see *it*)

**Rod**  abroad applaud awed broad clod cod defraud façade
fraud God guffawed Izod nod odd pod prod promenade
quad roughshod shod sod squad trod wad

**Rode**  (see **Road**)

**Roll**  bowl buttonhole cajole casserole coal control dole droll
enroll goal hole loophole Maypole mole Old King Cole
oriole parole patrol pole poll porthole role scroll tadpole
toll troll whole

**R**

**Roller**  bowler consoler controller molar polar solar
stroller troller

**Romance**  advance ants chance circumstance dance
enhance extravagance finance France glance lance
pants prance stance trance

**Romantic**  antic Atlantic chromatic frantic gigantic
pedantic transatlantic

**Roof**  aloof bulletproof goof hoof proof spoof
waterproof weatherproof

**Rookie**  bookie cooky hooky lookee

**Room**  bloom boom broom cloakroom doom entomb flume
gloom groom tomb whom womb zoom

**Roost**  boost

**Rooster**  booster (see *her*)

**Root**  (see **Shoot**)

**Rope**  antelope cantaloupe cope dope elope envelope grope
gyroscope hope horoscope kaleidoscope microscope
mope pope scope slope soap stethoscope telescope

**Rose**  arose chose close compose decompose depose
disclose dispose doze enclose expose foreclose froze
goes hose impose indispose interpose knows nose owes
pose predispose presuppose prose recompose suppose
those toes transpose woes

**R**

**Rosy**  cozy dozy mosey posy

**Rotate**  notate (see *ate*)

**Rotten**  begotten cotton gotten forgotten

**Rough**  bluff buff cuff duff enough fluff gruff huff muff powder
puff scruff scuff snuff stuff tough

**Rougher**  bluffer buffer duffer gruffer puffer suffer tougher

**Round**  abound around astound background battleground
bloodhound bound compound confound downed
dumbfound found ground hound impound

merry-go-round mound pound profound renowned
resound sound spellbound surround underground wound

**Roar**  (see **Door**)

**Routine**  (see **Mean**)

**Row**  (see **Blow**)

**Rowdy**  cloudy cum laude dowdy howdy

**Royal**  broil coil foil loyal oil recoil spoil toil turmoil

**Royalty**  loyalty (see *be*)

**Rub**  Beelzebub bub club cub grub hub hubbub pub
rub-a-dub-dub scrub shrub snub stub sub tub

**Ruby**  booby

**Rudder**  shudder udder

**Rude**  brood clued conclude crude dude exclude food
glued include intrude misconstrued mood preclude prude
seclude shrewd wooed

**Rule**  April fool cool drool fool ghoul Liverpool overrule pool
school spool stool tool whirlpool

**Ruler**  cooler drooler

**Rum**  (see **Dumb**)

**Rumor**  bloomer boomer consumer humor tumor

**Run**  anyone begun bun comparison done everyone fun
Galveston gun hon Hun jettison none nun oblivion one
outdone outrun overdone overrun phenomenon pun shun
simpleton skeleton son stun sun ton unison venison won

**Rung**  (see **Young**)

**Runner**  gunner stunner

**Rural**  extramural intramural mural neural plural

**Rush**  blush brush crush flush gush lush mush plush slush
thrush underbrush

**Rust**  adjust August bust crust disgust distrust encrust entrust
gust just lust mistrust must robust thrust trust unjust

**R**

# S

**Sack** almanac attack back black bric-a-brac Cadillac cardiac
clickety-clack egomaniac feedback hack Hackensack
haystack jack kleptomaniac knack lack maniac pack plaque
Pontiac prozac quack rack sack shack slack snack stack
tack track whack yak zodiac

**Sacrifice** advice concise device dice entice ice lice mice
nice paradise precise price rice spice splice suffice
thrice twice vice

**Sad** ad add bad Brad cad Chad clad Dad egad fad glad grad
had lad mad nomad pad plaid shad Trinidad

**Saddle** paddle straddle

**Safe** waif

**Sag** bag brag drag flag gag hag lag mag nag rag shag slag snag
stag swag tag wag

**Said** ahead bed bedspread bread bred coed dead dread fed
figurehead fled flowerbed fountainhead gingerbread head
inbred lead led misled misread overfed read red riverbed
shed shred sled sped spread thoroughbred thread
underfed unthread wed

**Sail** (see **Ale**)

**Sailor** inhaler jailer sailor staler trailer wailer whaler

**Saint** acquaint ain't complaint faint paint quaint restraint
taint 'tain't

**Salary** calorie gallery Mallory

**Saloon** (see **Moon**)

**Salt** assault cobalt exalt fault halt malt somersault vault

**Salty** faulty malty

**Same** acclaim aim became blame came claim exclaim
fame flame frame game inflame lame maim name
proclaim shame tame

**Sample**  ample example trample

**Sand**  and band brand canned command contraband demand
expand fanned grand hand land panned planned
reprimand Rio Grande stand

**Sandal**  candle dandle handle scandal vandal

**Sandy**  Andy brandy candy dandy handy randy

**Sang**  bang boomerang clang dang fang orangutan rang
slang sprang

**Sanity**  Christianity humanity insanity profanity vanity

**Sank**  bank blank clank crank dank drank flank frank
hank outrank plank prank rank shrank spank stank
tank thank yank

**Sappy**  crappie happy nappy pappy scrappy slaphappy yappy

**Sarcasm**  bioplasm chasm enthusiasm plasm spasm

**Sarcastic**  bombastic drastic elastic enthusiastic fantastic
gymnastic iconoclastic plastic scholastic spastic

**Sat**  (see **At**)

**Satisfactory**  factory refractory (see *story*)

**Savage**  lavage ravage scavage

**Save**  behave brave cave concave crave engrave forgave gave
grave knave pave rave shave slave waive wave

**Savior**  behavior misbehavior

**Saw**  Arkansas awe bra caw claw draw flaw gnaw guffaw hurrah    **S**
jaw law Ma macaw nah overdraw Pa paw raw seesaw shah
slaw squaw straw thaw withdraw

**Say**  array bay betray bluejay bouquet bray clay day decay
delay disarray dismay display eh? essay exposé fray gay
gray hay hey holiday hooray José Kay lay matinee may
moiré naysay negligée obey pay play portray protégé ray
résumé ricochet risqué rosé slay sleigh soufflé stay stray
sway they toupee way weigh x-ray

**Scald**   appalled bald

**Scandal**   candle dandle handle sandal vandal

**Scare**   (see **Air**)

**Scarf**   barf snarf

**Scary**   adversary airy arbitrary beneficiary berry bury canary
capillary cautionary cherry commentary culinary
customary dairy dictionary dietary dignitary disciplinary
discretionary evolutionary extraordinary fairy February
ferry functionary hairy hereditary honorary imaginary
incendiary intermediary January Jerry legendary legionary
literary luminary Mary mercenary military momentary
monetary mortuary nary necessary obituary ordinary
Perry planetary prairie proprietary pulmonary reactionary
revolutionary sanctuary sanitary secretary seminary
sherry solitary stationary temporary Terry Tipperary very
visionary vocabulary voluntary wary

**Scene**   (see **Seen**)

**Scenery**   beanery greenery machinery

**Scent**   absent accent augment cement comment compliment
consent content dent dissent ferment frequent indent
invent present prevent relent rent repent represent
resent supplement tent torment vent

**School**   April fool cool drool fool ghoul Liverpool overrule
pool rule spool stool tool whirlpool

**Scientific**   hieroglyphic horrific pacific prolific specific terrific

**Scope**   (see **Hope**)

**Score**   (see **Door**)

**Scorn**   adorn airborne born Cape Horn Capricorn corn
forlorn horn lovelorn Matterhorn morn mourn popcorn
stillborn sworn unicorn warn worn

S

**Scout**  about boy scout blow-out bout clout devout doubt
eke out flout gout lout out pout roundabout route shout
snout spout sprout stout tout trout wash-out worn-out

**Scramble**  amble gamble ramble shamble

**Scratch**  attach batch catch detach dispatch hatch latch
match patch snatch

**Scream**  beam cream deem dream esteem extreme gleam
ream regime scheme seam seen steam stream supreme
team teem

**Screw**  (see **Do**)

**Screwy**  buoy chewy dewy Drambuie gluey gooey hooey
Louie phooey St. Louie

**Script**  chipped dipped crypt equipped manuscript sipped
transcript whipped zipped

**Scrub**  Beelzebub bub club cub grub hub hubbub pub rub rub-
a-dub-dub shrub snub stub sub tub

**Scruple**  pupil

**Scuba**  Cuba tuba

**Scuffle**  duffle muffle ruffle shuffle truffle

**Scum**  album aquarium auditorium become bum burdensome
Christendom come cranium crematorium crumb
curriculum drum dump emporium fee-fi-fo-fum glum gum
gymnasium hum kettledrum kingdom martyrdom
maximum meddlesome medium millennium minimum
mum museum numb opium overcome pendulum
petroleum platinum plum premium quarrelsome radium
random rum sanitarium slum some strum succumb
sum swum tedium thumb Tom Thumb Tweedledum
uranium worrisome yum

**Sea**  (see **Be**)

S

**Seal** (see **Steal**)

**Search** besmirch birch church lurch perch research
search smirch

**Season** pleasin' reason sneezin' squeezin' teasin'
wheezin' (see *son*)

**Seat** (see **Sweet**)

**Secure** (see **Pure**)

**Seduce** abuse accuse confuse cues deduce diffuse disuse duce
excuse induce infuse introduce juice misuse obtuse peruse
produce profuse reduce refuse reproduce Syracuse use

**See** (see **Be**)

**Seed** agreed breed centipede concede creed deed exceed
feed greed heed inbreed knead lead mislead need precede
proceed read recede reed secede speed stampede
succeed Swede tweed weed

**Seeing** agreeing being decreeing disagreeing farseeing
fleeing foreseeing freeing guaranteeing overseeing
teeing unseeing

**Seek** beak bleak creek eek freak leak meek reek speak
tweak weak week

**Seen** bean between caffeine canteen chlorine clean codeine
Colleen convene cuisine dean demean evergreen
Florentine foreseen gasoline Gene green guillotine
Halloween in-between intervene kerosene lean lien
machine marine mean mezzanine Nazarene nectarine
nicotine obscene preen quarantine queen ravine routine
sardine scene serene spleen submarine tambourine
tangerine teen thirteen (etc.) Vaseline velveteen
wintergreen wolverine

**Self** elf herself himself itself myself shelf yourself

S

**Sell**  bell belle Carmel carrousel cell clientele dell dwell excel
       farewell fell gel hell hotel infidel knell mademoiselle
       personnel shell smell spell tell well yell

**Selling**  compelling dwelling excelling expelling
       foretelling fortune-telling misspelling quelling
       rebelling repelling shelling smelling spelling swelling
       telling underselling yelling

**Semester**  Chester contester fester investor jester
       Lester molester pester protester sequester tester
       Westchester Winchester

**Send**  apprehend ascend attend befriend bend blend commend
       comprehend condescend defend depend descend
       dividend end expend extend fend friend intend lend
       mend offend penned pretend recommend spend suspend
       tend transcend trend unbend

**Sensational**  congregational creational educational
       inspirational recreational representational

**Sense**  (see **Fence**)

**Sensed**  against condensed fenced

**Senses**  commences defenses dispenses fences offenses tenses

**Sensing**  condensing dispensing fencing
       incensing recompensing

**Sent**  (see **Bent**)

**Sentence**  repentance

**Sequel**  equal

**Serenity**  amenity obscenity

**Serial**  cereal immaterial material managerial ministerial

**Serious**  (see **Us**)

**Sermon**  determine German merman vermin

**Serve**  conserve curve deserve nerve observe preserve
       reserve swerve

**S**

**Settle** kettle metal mettle petal resettle settle

**Severe** (see **Near**)

**Sewer** bluer brewer doer fewer interviewer newer pursuer
reviewer skewer truer viewer wooer

**Sex** complex decks duplex ex flex necks pecks reflex
Rolidex specs Tex unisex

**Shack** (see **Sack)**

**Shackle** cackle crackle hackle ramshackle tackle

**Shade** (see **Afraid**)

**Shake** ache bake brake break cake fake flake forsake
headache heartache keepsake make mistake opaque
quake rake sake snake stake steak take wake

**Shall** canal chorale gal morale pal

**Shallow** callow fallow hallow mallow marshmallow tallow

**Sham** (see **Am**)

**Shamble** amble gamble ramble scramble

**Shame** acclaim aim became blame came claim exclaim
fame flame frame game inflame lame maim name
proclaim same tame

**Shanty** aunty panty scanty

**Shape** (see **Ape**)

**Shark** aardvark arc ark bark dark embark hark lark mark
narc park patriarch remark spark stark

**Sharp** carp harp

**She** (see **Be**)

**Shelf** elf herself himself itself myself self yourself

**Shelter** belter smelter swelter

**Shelve** delve twelve

**Shepherd** leopard peppered

**Shield** battlefield Chesterfield field wield yield

**S**

**Shift**  drift gift lift spendthrift swift thrift

**Shifty**  fifty nifty thrifty

**Shine**  align asinine assign benign combine concubine confine consign decline define design dine divine entwine fine incline line malign mine nine outshine pine porcupine recline refine resign Rhine shrine sign spine stein swine twine underline undermine vine whine wine

**Ship**  (see **Trip**)

**Shirt**  alert avert blurt concert convert curt desert dessert dirt divert exert expert extrovert flirt hurt insert introvert invert pervert skirt squirt subvert yogurt

**Shock**  Bangkok beanstalk boondock clock cock cornstalk crock deadlock defrock dock flintlock flock frock gawk gridlock hawk hock J. S. Bach jock knock Little Rock livestock lock mock Mohawk padlock peacock rock sidewalk small talk smock sock squawk stalk stock talk tomahawk unlock walk wok

**Shoe**  (see **Do**)

**Shoot**  absolute acute astute attribute beaut boot brute Butte chute commute compute constitute coot cute destitute dilute dispute disrepute dissolute electrocute enroute execute flute fruit hoot loot lute minute moot mute newt parachute persecute pollute prosecute prostitute pursuit recruit refute repute resolute root route scoot snoot substitute suit toot transmute uproot

**Shop**  (see **Drop**)

**Short**  abort assort cavort comfort contort court davenport deport distort escort exhort export extort fort import passport port quart report resort retort short snort sort sport support thwart tort transport wart

**S**

**Shot**  apricot blot Camelot clot cot cybot dot forget-me-not
forgot fought gavotte got hot hot-shot jot knot lot not
plot pot robot rot slingshot somewhat spot squat swat
tot trot watt what yacht

**Should**  brotherhood could fatherhood firewood good
Hollywood hood likelihood livelihood misunderstood
motherhood neighborhood sisterhood stood understood
withstood womanhood wood would

**Shout**  about boy scout blow-out bout clout devout doubt
eke out flout gout lout pout roundabout route scout
snout spout sprout stout tout trout wash-out worn-out

**Shove**  above dove glove ladylove love mourning dove
of turtle dove

**Shower**  cauliflower cower deflower empower flower
horsepower plower power tower (see *our*)

**Shown**  (see **Stone**)

**Shrank**  bank blank clank crank dank drank flank frank
hank outrank plank prank rank sank spank stank
tank thank yank

**Shrewd**  brood clued conclude crude dude exclude food
glued include intrude misconstrued mood preclude
prude rude seclude wooed

**Shrewdly**  crudely lewdly rudely

**Shrimp**  blimp gimp limp pimp skimp wimp

**Shrine**  (see **Fine**)

**Shrink**  blink brink chink clink drink fink ink kink link mink
pink rink sink slink stink wink zinc

**Shroud**  allowed aloud cloud crowd enshroud loud plowed
proud thundercloud

**Shuffle**  duffle muffle ruffle truffle

**Shut**  but butt cut glut gut halibut hut King Tut mutt nut putt
rut scuttlebutt smut strut uncut

**Shy**  (see **Cry**)

**Shyly**  dryly highly Reilly slyly spryly wily wryly

**Sick**  arithmetic arsenic brick candlestick candlewick Catholic
chick click flick heartsick hick kick lick limerick love-sick
lunatic maverick nick pick slick stick thick tic tick wick

**Side**  beside bonafide bride collide confide countryside decide
defied died dignified divide eyed fireside guide hide hillside
homicide inside lied outside override pride provide reside
ride slide snide stride subdivide subside suicide tide tried
wide yuletide

**Sight**  appetite bite blight bright byte contrite copyright
daylight delight despite dynamite excite Fahrenheit
fight flight fright headlight height ignite invite kite
knight light midnight might moonlight night outright
parasite plight polite quite recite reunite right satellite
site sleight slight spite starlight sunlight tight trite
twilight unite white write

**Sign**  align asinine assign benign combine concubine confine
consign decline define design dine divine entwine fine
incline line malign mine nine outshine pine porcupine
recline refine resign Rhine shine shrine spine stein swine
twine underline undermine vine whine wine

**Signature**  (see **Pure**)

**Signify**  dignify (see *cry*)

**Silk**  bilk ilk milk

**Silly**  Billy Chile Chili chilly dilly filly frilly hillbilly hilly lily Philly
Piccadilly piccalilli shrilly willy-nilly

**Simmer**  dimmer glimmer grimmer primmer skimmer
slimmer swimmer trimmer

**Simple**  dimple pimple

**Sin**  aspirin been begin Berlin bin chagrin chin discipline feminine fin genuine gin grin harlequin heroine in inn kin mandolin mannequin masculine moccasin origin pin saccharine shin skin spin thick-and-thin thin tin twin violin within win

**Since**  convince hints mints prince rinse wince

**Sincere**  (see **Near**)

**Sincerity**  austerity dexterity insincerity posterity prosperity severity

**Sing**  anything bring cling ding evening everything fling king ring sling spring sting string swing thing wing wring (add "ing" to "action" words, i.e., run(ning), etc.)

**Single**  intermingle jingle Kris Kringle mingle shingle tingle

**Sink**  blink brink chink clink drink fink ink kink link mink pink rink shrink slink stink think wink zinc

**Sinner**  B. F. Skinner beginner breadwinner dinner inner skinner spinner thinner winner

**Sinister**  administer minister

**Siphon**  hyphen

**Sir**  (see **Her**)

**Sirloin**  purloin

**S**

**Sister**  assister blister magister mister resister twister (see *her*)

**Sit**  befit bit fit 'git grit kit knit hit it lit mitt nit-wit pit quit twit unfit ultimate wit zit

**Size**  (see **Lies**)

**Sizzle**  chisel drizzle fizzle frizzle grizzle swizzle

**Skate**  (see **Ate**)

**Skeptic**  antiseptic septic

**Sketch**  catch etch fetch kvetch retch stretch wretch

**Skid**  bid did forbid grid hid invalid lid Madrid pyramid
rid slid squid

**Skin**  (see **Been**)

**Skinny**  New Guinea ninny tinny

**Skirt**  (see **Shirt**)

**Skull**  annul cull dull gull hull lull mull scull

**Skunk**  bunk chunk clunk cyberpunk drunk dunk flunk funk
hunk junk monk plunk punk shrunk slunk spunk stunk
sunk trunk

**Sky**  (see **Cry**)

**Skyscraper**  caper draper escaper paper scraper shaper taper

**Slacker**  attacker backer blacker cracker hacker hijacker
nutcracker packer ransacker smacker tracker

**Slam**  (see **Am**)

**Slang**  bang boomerang clang dang fang orangutan
rang sang sprang

**Slant**  (see **Ant**)

**Slap**  cap chap clap flap gap handicap lap map mishap nap rap
sap scrap snap strap tap trap wrap zap

**Slaughter**  blotter daughter hotter otter plotter spotter
squatter trotter water

**Slave**  behave brave cave concave crave engrave forgave gave
grave knave pave rave save shave waive wave

**Slavery**  (see **Be**)

**Sleaze**  (see **Ease**)

**Sled**  (see **Said**)

**Sleep**  barkeep cheep creep deep heap keep leap peep reap
seep sheep steep sweep weep

**S**

**Sleeve**  achieve believe bereave conceive disbelieve
eve grieve heave leave perceive receive relieve
reprieve retrieve weave

**Sleigh**  (see **Say**)

**Slept**  accept adept crept except intercept kept overslept
stepped swept wept

**Sleuth**  booth couth Duluth tooth truth uncouth youth

**Slid**  bid did forbid grid hid invalid lid Madrid pyramid
rid skid squid

**Slim**  brim dim grim gym hymn limb pseudonym skim
swim trim whim

**Slime**  chime climb crime dime I'm lime mime pantomime
prime rhyme summertime thyme time

**Slob**  blob bob cob fob gob hob hobnob job knob lob mob
nob rob snob sob swab throb

**Sloppy**  choppy copy floppy hoppy poppy soppy

**Slow**  (see **Blow**)

**Slum**  (see **Scum**)

**Slumber**  cucumber cumber encumber lumber
number umber

**Small**  all ball bawl brawl call crawl doll drawl fall gall haul
install mall maul Montreal nightfall overhaul parasol
pitfall protocol rainfall scrawl shawl snowfall sprawl
stall tall thrall wall waterfall y'all

**Smart**  apart art cart chart counterpart dart depart heart
mart part start sweetheart tart upstart

**Smash**  ash balderdash bash brash cash clash crash dash flash
gnash rash rehash slash splash stash thrash trash

**Smell**  bell belle Carmel carrousel cell clientele dell dwell

**S**

excel farewell fell gel hell hotel infidel knell mademoiselle
personnel sell shell spell tell well yell

**Smile**  aisle awhile beguile bile compile crocodile defile file isle
juvenile meanwhile mile Nile pile rile style tile vile while
wile worthwhile

**Smiling**  beguiling compiling defiling filing piling reconciling
reviling styling tiling

**Smirk**  clerk handiwork irk jerk Kirk lurk murk overwork
perk quirk shirk Turk work

**Smoke**  (see **Joke**)

**Smooch**  hooch mooch pooch

**Smooth**  soothe

**Smudge**  budge drudge fudge grudge judge misjudge nudge

**Smug**  bug drug dug jug hug lug mug plug pug rug shrug slug
snug thug tug

**Smuggle**  juggle snuggle struggle

**Smut**  (see **But**)

**Snack**  (see **Sack**)

**Snake**  ache bake brake break cake fake flake forsake
headache heartache keepsake make mistake opaque
quake rake sake shake stake steak take wake

**Sniff**  cliff handkerchief if stiff tiff whiff

**Sniffle**  piffle riffle whiffle

**Snivel**  civil drivel shrivel swivel

**Snob**  blob bob cob fob gob hob hobnob job knob lob mob
nob rob slob sob swab throb

**Snow**  (see **Blow**)

**Snowy**  blowy Bowie doughy showy

S

**So**   afro although banjo beau below bestow blow bow buffalo bungalow calico crossbow crow depot doe domino dough embryo escrow Eskimo flow foe forgo fro gazebo gigolo glow go grow heigh-ho ho-ho hobo hoe incognito indigo Joe know long ago low Mexico mistletoe mow no oboe oh outgrow overflow overgrow overthrow owe Pinocchio pistachio plateau quo rainbow ratio roe row sew slow snow Soho status quo stow studio tally-ho though throw tiptoe to-and-fro toe Tokyo tow tremolo undergo undertow vertigo woe yo yo-yo

**Soap**   (see **Hope**)

**Sob**   blob bob cob fob gob hob hobnob job knob lob mob nob rob slob snob swab throb

**Sober**   disrober October prober rober

**Society**   anxiety impropriety notoriety piety propriety sobriety variety

**Sock**   (see **Shock**)

**Soda**   coda pagoda

**Soft**   aloft loft oft

**Sold**   behold blindfold bold centerfold cold fold foothold foretold gold hold household marigold mold old retold scold told uphold withhold

**Solitaire**   (see **Air**)

**Solitary**   (see **Scary**)

**Solitude**   allude altitude aptitude attitude delude dude feud fortitude gratitude interlude latitude lewd longitude magnitude multitude nude prelude pursued renewed subdued sued 'tude you'd

**Solo**   bolo coco gigolo piccolo polo tremolo

**Solution**   (see **Revolution**)

**Solve**   absolve devolve dissolve evolve involve revolve

**Some** (see **Scum**)

**Some** album aquarium auditorium become bum burdensome
Christendom come cranium crematorium crumb
curriculum drum dumb emporium fee-fi-fo-fum glum gum
gymnasium hum kettledrum kingdom martyrdom
maximum meddlesome medium millennium minimum
mum museum numb opium overcome pendulum
petroleum platinum plum premium quarrelsome radium
random rum sanitarium scum slum strum succumb
sum swum tedium thumb Tom Thumb Tweedledum
uranium worrisome yum

**Somebody** body embody gaudy lawdy nobody shoddy toddy

**Son** anyone begun bun comparison done everyone fun
Galveston gun hon Hun jettison none nun oblivion one
outdone outrun overdone overrun phenomenon pun run
shun simpleton skeleton stun sun ton unison venison won

**Song** along belong bong ding-dong gong Hong Kong long
Ping-Pong prong strong throng wrong

**Soon** afternoon baboon balloon bassoon boon buffoon
cartoon cocoon coon croon goon harpoon harvest moon
honeymoon lagoon lampoon loon maroon monsoon
moon noon platoon prune raccoon saloon Saskatoon
spittoon swoon tycoon typhoon (see *tune*)

**Soothe** smooth

**Sorrow** borrow morrow sorrow tomorrow

**Sought** (see **Thought**)

**Sound** abound around astound background battleground
bloodhound bound compound confound downed
dumbfound found ground hound impound merry-go-
round mound pound profound renowned resound round
spellbound surround underground wound

**S**

**Soup**  coop droop dupe group hoop loop nincompoop poop
scoop sloop stoop swoop troop troupe whoop

**Source**  coarse course divorce endorse force horse Norse
reinforce remorse resource

**Space**  ace  base bass brace case chase commonplace debase
disgrace displace embrace encase erase face grace lace
mace misplace pace place race replace steeplechase trace
unlace vase

**Spare**  (see **Air**)

**Spark**  aardvark arc ark bark dark embark hark lark mark
narc park patriarch remark shark stark

**Sparrow**  arrow barrow harrow marrow narrow tarot

**Sparse**  farce parse

**Spasm**  bioplasm chasm enthusiasm plasm sarcasm

**Spat**  (see **At**)

**Speak**  beak bleak creek eek freak leak meek reek seek
tweak weak week

**Speech**  beach breach each impeach leech peach preach
reach screech teach

**Speed**  agreed breed centipede concede creed deed exceed
feed greed heed inbreed knead lead mislead need precede
proceed read recede reed secede seed stampede succeed
Swede tweed weed

**Spent**  (see **Bent**)

**Sperm**  affirm confirm firm germ reaffirm squirm term worm

**Spider**  chider cider decider divider glider insider low-rider
outsider provider rider slider wider

**Splash**  ash balderdash bash brash cash clash crash dash flash
gnash rash rehash slash smash stash thrash trash

**Splendor**  (see **Tender**)

**Spoil**  broil coil foil loyal oil recoil royal toil turmoil

S

**Spoken** broken heartbroken Hoboken jokin' oaken
outspoken smokin' soakin' token

**Sponge** lunge plunge

**Spook** fluke kook

**Spooky** fluky kooky pooky

**Sport** (see **Short**)

**Spot** (see **Pot**)

**Spouse** blouse douse grouse house louse madhouse mouse
outhouse penthouse slaughterhouse souse

**Sprang** bang boomerang clang dang fang orangutan
rang sang slang

**Sprinkle** crinkle periwinkle tinkle twinkle wrinkle

**Spurn** (see **Learn**)

**Squabble** bobble cobble gobble hobble wobble

**Squalor** bawler brawler call 'er caller choler collar crawler
dollar hauler mauler scrawler smaller taller

**Squander** condor conned 'er fonder launder ponder
wander yonder

**Square** (see **Air**)

**Squeeze** (see **Ease**)

**Squish** devilish dish fish gibberish impoverish swish wish

**Stab** blab cab crab dab drab gab grab jab lab nab scab tab

**Stack** (see **Sack**)

**Staff** calf carafe epitaph giraffe graph laugh paragraph
phonograph photograph polygraph riffraff telegraph

**Stage** age cage gage page rampage sage wage

**Stagger** bagger bragger carpet-bagger dagger swagger tagger

**Stale** (see **Ale**)

**Stall** all ball bawl brawl call crawl doll drawl fall gall haul install
mall maul Montreal nightfall overhaul parasol pitfall
protocol rainfall scrawl shawl small snowfall sprawl tall
thrall wall waterfall y'all

**S**

**Stallion**  battalion Italian medallion rapscallion scallion

**Stamp**  amp camp champ clamp cramp damp lamp ramp vamp

**Stand**  and band brand canned command contraband demand
expand fanned grand hand land panned planned
reprimand Rio Grande sand

**Stank**  bank blank clank crank dank drank flank frank
hank outrank plank prank rank sank shrank spank
tank thank yank

**Stanza**  bonanza extravaganza

**Staple**  maple papal

**Star**  are bar bazaar bizarre car caviar cigar czar disbar far
guitar jar par scar spar tar

**Starch**  arch march parch

**Stare**  (see **Air**)

**Start**  apart art cart chart counterpart dart depart heart mart
part smart sweetheart tart upstart

**Starve**  carve

**Static**  (see **Attic**)

**Stay**  (see **Say**)

**Steal**  appeal automobile Bastille Camille conceal deal eel feel
genteel he'll heal heel ideal kneel meal mobile peel real
reel repeal reveal seal she'll spiel squeal steel veal we'll
wheel zeal

**S**

**Steel**  (see **Steal**)

**Stem**  Bethlehem condemn gem hem phlegm requiem them

**Step**  footstep pep rep

**Stew**  (see **Do**)

**Stick**  (see **Pick**)

**Still**  bill chill daffodil distill drill fill frill fulfill gill grill hill ill
imbecile instill kill mill nil quill shrill sill skill spill swill thrill
till trill until whippoorwill will windmill windowsill

**Stink**  blink brink chink clink drink fink ink kink link mink pink
rink shrink sink slink wink zinc

**Stir**  (see **Her**)

**Stirrup**  chirrup syrup (see *up*)

**Stolen**  colon rollin' semicolon (see *in*)

**Stomp**  comp pomp romp swamp tromp

**Stone**  alone atone backbone baritone blown bone chaperone
clone condone cone cornerstone cyclone Dictaphone
flown full-blown full-grown gramophone grindstone groan
grown headstone known loan lone microphone milestone
moan monotone mown overgrown overthrown own
phone postpone prone saxophone sewn shown telephone
thrown tone trombone unknown xylophone zone

**Stood**  brotherhood could fatherhood firewood good
Hollywood hood likelihood livelihood misunderstood
motherhood neighborhood should sisterhood understood
withstood womanhood wood would

**Stop**  chop cop crop drop eavesdrop flop hop lollipop mop
plop pop prop raindrop shop swap tip-top whop

**Store**  (see **Door**)

**Stork**  cork fork New York pitchfork pork torque uncork

**Storm**  chloroform conform deform form inform norm
perform rainstorm reform snowstorm swarm transform
uniform warm

**S**

**Story**  accusatory allegory category dormitory dory glory
gory hunky-dory laboratory Lori obligatory observatory
oratory Peter Lorre quarry reformatory retaliatory sorry
story territory Tory

**Strange**  arrange change derange estrange exchange range

**Strangle**  angle dangle entangle jangle mangle spangle tangle
triangle wrangle

**Stream**  beam cream deem dream esteem extreme gleam
    ream regime scheme scream seam seen steam supreme
    team teem

**Street**  (see **Sweet**)

**Strength**  length

**Stress**  (see **Confess**)

**Stricken**  chicken quicken sicken thicken (see *in*)

**Strict**  addict conflict constrict contradict convict derelict
    evict flicked inflict licked predict pricked

**Strike**  bike hike like mike spike tyke

**Strong**  along belong bong ding-dong gong Hong Kong long
    Ping-Pong prong song throng wrong

**Stronger**  longer

**Struck**  amuck buck chuck cluck deduct duck horror-struck
    luck muck pluck potluck puck suck truck tuck

**Struggle**  juggle smuggle snuggle

**Strum**  (see **Scum**)

**Strung**  (see **Young**)

**Strut**  (see **But**)

**Stud**  blood bud cud dud flood mud scud spud thud

**Stuff**  (see **Bluff**)

**Stuffy**  fluffy huffy puffy

**Stump**  bump chump clump dump hump jump lump plump
    rump slump thump trump ump

**Stunk**  bunk chunk clunk cyberpunk drunk dunk flunk funk
    hunk junk monk plunk punk shrunk skunk slunk spunk
    sunk trunk

**Stunt**  affront blunt brunt bunt confront forefront front grunt
    hunt punt runt shunt

**Stupid**  Cupid

**S**

**Style**  (see **Smile**)

**Subject**  (see **Defect**)

**Subtle**  cuttle rebuttal scuttle shuttle (see *puddle*)

**Suburb**  blurb 'burb curb disturb herb perturb Serb
superb verb

**Such**  clutch crutch Dutch hutch inasmuch much
retouch touch

**Suck**  amuck buck chuck cluck deduct duck horror-struck luck
muck pluck potluck puck struck truck tuck

**Sue**  (see **Knew**)

**Suffer**  bluffer buffer duffer gruffer puffer rougher tougher

**Suggestion**  congestion digestion indigestion
ingestion question

**Suicidal**  bridal bridle homicidal idle idol tidal

**Suit**  (see **Shoot**)

**Suite**  (see **Sweet**)

**Suitor**  commuter computer cuter muter neuter persecutor
polluter prosecutor tutor

**Sulk**  bulk hulk

**Summer**  comer drummer dumber hummer
newcomer strummer

**Sun**  (see **Son**)

**Sung**  among clung dung flung high-strung hung lung rung
slung sprung strung stung swung tongue unstrung unsung
wrung young

**Sunk**  bunk chunk clunk cyberpunk drunk dunk flunk funk
hunk junk monk plunk punk shrunk skunk slunk spunk
stunk trunk

**Sunny**  bunny funny honey money

**Sunrise**  (see **Lies**)

**S**

**Sunset**  alphabet bayonet bet brunette cabinet cadet cigarette
clarinet cornet corvette debt duet forget fret gazette get
jet Joliet Juliet let luncheonette marionette met net
omelet pet quartet regret roulette set silhouette
Somerset sweat threat Tibet toilette upset vet 'vette
violet wet yet

**Super**  cooper hooper looper snooper stupor trooper

**Superb**  blurb 'burb curb disturb herb perturb Serb
suburb verb

**Superficial**  artificial beneficial initial judicial official sacrificial

**Superior**  exterior inferior interior ulterior

**Superstition**  (see **Tradition**)

**Supper**  upper

**Supportive**  (See **Abortive**)

**Sure**  allure armature assure brochure caricature cocksure
cure demure endure ensure expenditure immature
impure insecure insure liqueur literature lure manicure
manure mature miniature obscure overture pedicure
premature pure reassure secure signature tablature
temperature your

**Surf**  nerf serf turf

**Surge**  (see **Verge**)

**Surgeon**  burgeon emergin' mergin' sturgeon surgin'
urgin' virgin

**Surgery**  perjury

**Survival**  arrival revival rival

**Suspect**  (see **Defect**)

**Suspected**  affected bisected corrected defected deflected
detected directed disaffected dissected effected erected
expected infected inflected inspected intersected
neglected objected perfected protected reflected
respected resurrected unaffected unexpected

S

**Suspicious**  (see **Vicious**)

**Swagger**  carpetbagger dagger stagger

**Swallow**  Apollo follow hollow wallow

**Swam** (see **Am**)

**Swamp**  prompt stomp

**Swan**  Amazon Babylon begone bonbon Bonn brawn chiffon
con Don dawn drawn fawn gone hexagon John lawn
lexicon octagon on Oregon pawn pentagon silicon
undergone upon withdrawn wanton yawn

**Swear**  affair air anywhere aware bare bear billionaire blare
care chair compare dare debonair declare despair
disrepair elsewhere everywhere fair fare flair glare hair
hare heir impair legionnaire mare midair millionaire
nightmare pair pare pear Pierre prayer prepare rare
ready-to-wear repair scare snare solitaire somewhere
spare square stair stare tear their there thoroughfare
unaware underwear unfair ware wear where

**Sweat**  (see **Sunset**)

**Sweater**  better debtor getter letter setter wetter

**Sweet**  athlete beat beet bittersweet bleat cheat compete
complete conceit concrete deceit defeat delete deplete
discreet discrete eat elite feat feet fleet greet heat
incomplete indiscreet meat meet mistreat neat obsolete
parakeet receipt repeat retreat seat sheet sleet street
suite treat wheat

**Sweetly**  completely concretely discreetly indiscreetly
fleetly neatly

**Sweety**  meaty treaty

**Swept**  accept adept crept except intercept kept overslept
slept stepped wept

**Swift**  drift gift lift shift spendthrift thrift

**S**

**Swig**  big dig fig gig jig pig rig thingamajig twig wig

**Swim**  brim dim grim gym hymn limb pseudonym skim slim trim whim

**Swindle**  dwindle kindle rekindle spindle

**Swing**  (see **Sing**)

**Swipe**  archetype gripe hype pipe prototype ripe stereotype stripe type wipe

**Swirl**  curl earl girl hurl pearl twirl whirl

**Switch**  bewitch bitch ditch enrich glitch hitch pitch rich snitch stitch twitch which

**Swollen**  bowlin' rollin' stolen

**Swamp**  comp pomp romp stomp tromp

**Sword**  aboard accord afford award board bored ford harpsichord hoard lord overboard poured reward shuffleboard soared ward

**Swore**  (see **Door**)

**Syllable**  fillable tillable

**Symbol**  cymbal nimble thimble

**S**

# T

**Tab**  blab cab crab dab drab gab grab jab lab nab scab slab stab
**Table**  (see **Able**)
**Tackle**  cackle crackle hackle ramshackle shackle
**Tad**  (see **Mad**)
**Tag**  bag brag drag flag gag hag lag mag nag rag sag shag slag
    snag stag swag wag
**Take**  ache bake brake break cake fake flake forsake headache
    heartache keepsake make mistake opaque quake rake
    shake snake stake steak wake
**Taken**  achin' bacon fakin' forsaken Jamaican makin' mistaken
    overtaken shaken undertaken unshaken waken
**Talk**  Bangkok beanstalk boondock cock cornstalk clock crock
    deadlock defrock dock flintlock flock frock gawk gridlock
    hawk hock J. S. Bach jock knock Little Rock livestock lock
    mock Mohawk padlock peacock rock shock sidewalk
    small smock sock squawk stalk stock tomahawk unlock
    walk wok
**Tall**  all ball bawl brawl call crawl doll drawl fall gall haul install
    mall maul Montreal nightfall overhaul parasol pitfall
    protocol rainfall scrawl shawl small snowfall sprawl stall
    thrall wall waterfall y'all
**Tame**  (see **Aim**)
**Tangle**  angle dangle entangle jangle mangle spangle strangle
    triangle wrangle
**Tango**  fandango mango
**Tank**  bank blank clank crank dank drank flank frank
    hank outrank plank prank rank sank shrank spank stank
    thank yank

**T**

**Tap**  cap chap clap flap gap handicap lap map mishap nap rap
sap scrap slap snap strap trap wrap zap

**Tape**  (see **Ape**)

**Tarnish**  garnish varnish

**Tarot**  arrow barrow harrow marrow narrow sparrow

**Task**  ask bask cask flask mask masque

**Taste**  baste aftertaste braced chaste distaste faced freckle-
faced haste hatchet-faced lambaste paste waist waste

**Tattoo**  (see **Do**)

**Tavern**  cavern

**Tax**  ax backs fax jacks lax max relax packs Saks
sax slacks wax

**Taxes**  axes battle-axes relaxes saxes waxes

**Tea**  (see **Be**)

**Teach**  beach breach each impeach leech peach preach
reach screech speech

**Teacher**  bleacher creature feature preacher screecher

**Team**  beam cream deem dream esteem extreme gleam
ream regime scheme scream seam seen steam stream
supreme teem

**Tear**  adhere appear atmosphere auctioneer beer bombardier
career cashier cavalier chandelier cheer clear dear
deer disappear ear engineer fear financier frontier gear
hear hemisphere here insincere interfere jeer lavaliere
leer mere mountaineer near overhear overseer peer
persevere pioneer queer racketeer reappear rear revere
seer severe shear sheer sincere smear sneer spear sphere
stratosphere veneer volunteer year

**Tearful**  cheerful earful fearful

**Tease**  (see **Ease**)

**Tedium**  medium (see *some*)

**T**

**Teeny**  Bellini fettucini genie meany Mussolini
   scaloppini weenie

**Teeth**  beneath heath teeth underneath wreath

**Telegram**  (see **Am**)

**Television**  (see **Vision**)

**Tell**  bell belle Carmel carrousel cell clientele dell dwell excel
   farewell fell gel hell hotel infidel knell mademoiselle
   personnel sell shell smell spell well yell

**Temperature**  (see **Pure**)

**Tempt**  attempt contempt dreamt exempt unkempt

**Tempted**  attempted exempted pre-empted

**Tender**  bender blender contender defender extender
   fender gender lender mender offender pretender
   sender slender spender splendor surrender suspender
   vendor weekender

**Tennis**  menace

**Tense**  (see **Fence**)

**Tension**  abstention apprehension ascension attention
   comprehension condescension convention dissension
   detention dimension dissension extension intention
   intervention invention mention retention suspension

**Term**  affirm confirm firm germ reaffirm sperm squirm worm

**Terrific**  hieroglyphic horrific pacific prolific scientific specific

**Terror**  bearer carer darer error wearer

**T**

**Testimony**  acrimony alimony baloney bony crony
   macaroni matrimony patrimony phony pony
   sanctimony stony Tony

**Text**  context flexed next pretext

**Thank**  bank blank clank crank dank drank flank frank
   hank outrank plank prank rank sank shrank spank
   stank tank yank

**Thankful**  tankful (see *bull*)

**Thaw**  (see **Draw**)

**Theft**  deft left

**Them**  Bethlehem condemn gem hem phlegm requiem stem

**Then**  amen citizen den fen hen hydrogen Ken oxygen pen
regimen specimen ten yen zen

**Theory**  teary weary (see *be*)

**There**  affair air anywhere aware bare bear billionaire blare
care chair compare dare debonair declare despair
disrepair elsewhere everywhere fair fare flair glare hair
hare heir impair legionnaire mare midair millionaire
nightmare pair pare pear Pierre prayer prepare rare
ready-to-wear repair scare snare solitaire somewhere
spare square stair stare swear tear their thoroughfare
unaware underwear unfair ware wear where

**Thick**  arithmetic arsenic brick candlestick candlewick
Catholic chick click flick heartsick hick kick lick
limerick love-sick lunatic maverick nick pick sick
slick stick tic tick wick

**Thief**  beef belief brief chief disbelief grief leaf relief

**Thin**  (see **Been**)

**Thing**  (see **Sing**)

**Think**  blink brink chink clink drink fink ink kink link mink
pink rink shrink sink slink stink wink zinc

**Thirst**  burst cursed first nursed outburst versed worst

**This**  abyss amiss analysis armistice bliss carcass cowardice
dismiss emphasis hiss hypothesis kiss miss nemesis
prejudice Swiss synthesis

**Thorough**  borough burrow furrow

**Thought**  astronaut bought brought caught cosmonaut fought
naught ought overwrought sought taught wrought

**T**

**Threat**  (see **Sunset**)

**Thrill**  bill chill daffodil distill drill fill frill fulfill gill grill hill
ill imbecile instill kill mill nil quill shrill sill skill spill still
swill till trill until whippoorwill will windmill windowsill

**Thriller**  caterpillar chiller distiller driller filler instiller killer
pillar shriller spiller swiller tiller

**Throat**  afloat antidote bloat boat coat connote denote
dote float footnote gloat goat misquote moat note oat
overcoat promote quote remote riverboat rote smote
tote underwrote vote wrote

**Throb**  blob bob cob gob hob hobnob job knob lob mob nob
rob slob snob sob

**Throw**  (see **Blow**)

**Thrown**  alone atone backbone baritone blown bone
chaperone clone condone cone cornerstone cyclone
Dictaphone flown full-blown full-grown gramophone
grindstone groan grown headstone known loan lone
microphone milestone moan monotone mown
overgrown overthrown own phone postpone prone
saxophone sewn shown stone telephone tone trombone
unknown xylophone zone

**Thrust**  (see **Trust**)

**Thumb**  album aquarium auditorium become bum
burdensome Christendom come cranium crematorium
crumb curriculum dumb drum emporium fee-fi-fo-fum
glum gum gymnasium hum kettledrum kingdom
martyrdom maximum meddlesome medium millennium
minimum mum museum numb opium overcome
pendulum petroleum platinum plum premium
quarrelsome radium random rum sanitarium scum
slum some strum succumb sum swum tedium Tom Thumb
Tweedledum uranium worrisome yum

**T**

**Thunder**  blunder plunder under wonder

**Thus**  (see **Us**)

**Tick**  arithmetic arsenic brick candlestick candlewick
Catholic chick click flick heartsick hick kick lick
limerick love-sick lunatic maverick nick pick sick
slick stick thick tic wick

**Ticket**  cricket picket thicket wicket (see *it*)

**Ticking**  bricking clicking flicking kicking licking pricking
slicking sticking

**Tide**  beside bonafide bride collide confide countryside decide
defied died dignified divide eyed fireside guide hide hillside
homicide inside lied outside override pride provide reside
ride side slide snide stride subdivide subside suicide tried
wide yuletide

**Tight**  (see **Write**)

**Tilt**  built guilt hilt jilt kilt quilt spilt stilt Vanderbilt wilt

**Time**  chime climb crime dime I'm lime mime pantomime
prime rhyme slime summertime thyme

**Tingle**  intermingle jingle Kris Kringle mingle shingle single

**Tint**  flint hint lint mint peppermint print spearmint splint
sprint squint

**Tip**  battleship chip clip dip drip equip flip grip gyp hip lip nip
quip rip scrip ship slip snip strip trip whip zip

**Tipsy**  dipsy gypsy Poughkeepsie

**Tire**  (see **Fire**)

**Tissue**  issue (see *you*)

**Titanic**  (see **Volcanic**)

**Title**  entitle recital vital

**Tizzy**  busy dizzy frizzy Lizzie tin lizzie

**To**  (see **Do**)

**Toad**  (see **Road**)

**Toast**  boast coast foremost furthermost ghost host
innermost most post roast whipping post

**Toga**  Saratoga yoga

**Together**  altogether feather Heather leather tether
weather whether (see *her*)

**Toggle**  boggle boondoggle goggle

**Toil**  broil coil foil loyal oil recoil royal spoil turmoil

**Told**  behold blindfold bold centerfold cold fold foothold
foretold gold hold household marigold mold old retold
scold sold uphold withhold

**Toll**  (see **Roll**)

**Tomorrow**  borrow morrow sorrow

**Ton**  anyone begun bun comparison done everyone fun
Galveston gun hon Hun jettison none nun oblivion
one outdone outrun overdone overrun phenomenon
pun run shun simpleton skeleton son stun sun ton
unison venison won

**Tongue**  (see **Young**)

**Tonic**  catatonic chronic diatonic enharmonic harmonic
ironic monophonic philharmonic phonic platonic
polyphonic sonic symphonic

**Took**  book brook cook crook hook look mistook nook
outlook rook shook undertook

**Tool**  April fool cool drool fool ghoul Liverpool overrule pool
rule school spool stool whirlpool

**Tooth**  booth couth Duluth sleuth truth uncouth youth

**Torch**  porch scorch

**Tornado**  bravado Colorado desperado El Dorado
Laredo Mikado

**Toss**  across albatross boss cross double-cross floss gloss loss
moss rhinoceros sauce

**Total**  anecdotal antidotal

**Touch**  clutch crutch Dutch hutch inasmuch much
      retouch such

**Touches**  clutches crutches

**Tough**  bluff buff cuff duff enough fluff gruff huff muff powder
      puff rough scruff scuff snuff stuff

**Towel**  bowel dowel trowel vowel

**Tower**  cauliflower cower deflower empower flower
      horsepower plower power shower (see *our, her*)

**Town**  brown clown crown down downtown drown
      frown gown hand-me-down noun renown tumble-down
      upside down uptown

**Toy**  ahoy annoy boy buoy convoy corduroy coy decoy
      destroy employ enjoy Illinois joy ploy Roy Savoy soy
      troy viceroy

**Trace**  (see **Space**)

**Tracer**  ace 'er eraser face 'er pacer place 'er (see *her*)

**Track**  almanac attack back black bric-a-brac Cadillac cardiac
      clickety-clack egomaniac feedback hack Hackensack
      haystack jack kleptomaniac knack lack maniac pack plaque
      Pontiac prozac quack rack sack shack slack snack stack
      tack whack yak zodiac

**Traction**  (see **Action**)

**T** **Trade**  (see **Afraid**)

**Tradition**  acquisition addition admission ambition
      ammunition attrition audition coalition commission
      competition composition condition definition demolition
      deposition disposition edition electrician emission
      exhibition expedition exposition extradition fission
      ignition imposition inhibition inquisition intermission
      intuition magician mathematician mission musician
      nutrition omission opposition partition permission

petition physician politician position prohibition
proposition recognition rendition repetition requisition
statistician submission superstition technician
transmission transposition transition tuition (see *in*)

**Tragic**  magic

**Trailer**  inhaler jailer sailor staler wailer whaler

**Train**  abstain again airplane arraign ascertain attain brain Cain
campaign cane chain champagne cocaine complain contain
crane detain disdain domain drain entertain explain
feign gain grain humane hurricane hydroplane insane
lane main Maine maintain mane migraine obtain ordain
pain pane pertain plain plane profane propane rain refrain
reign rein remain sane slain Spain sprain stain strain
sustain vain vane vein wane windowpane

**Trait**  (see **Ate**)

**Trance**  advance ants chance circumstance dance enhance
extravagance finance France glance lance pants prance
romance stance

**Transplant**  (see *Ant*)

**Trap**  cap chap clap flap gap handicap lap map mishap nap rap
sap scrap slap snap strap tap wrap zap

**Trapeze**  (see **Ease**)

**Trash**  ash balderdash bash brash cash clash crash dash flash
gnash rash rehash slash smash splash stash thrash

**T**

**Traumatic**  (see **Attic**)

**Travel**  gavel gravel ravel unravel

**Treasure**  displeasure measure pleasure

**Treat**  (see **Sweet**)

**Tree**  (see **Be**)

**Tremendous**  horrendous stupendous (see *us*)

**Trench**  bench clench drench French monkey wrench quench
stench wench wrench

**Trend**  (see **Friend**)

**Trial**  denial dial retrial self-denial viol

**Triangle**  angle dangle entangle jangle mangle spangle strangle
tangle wrangle

**Tribe**  bribe circumscribe describe jibe prescribe
scribe subscribe

**Trigger**  bigger chigger digger rigger rigor swigger tigger vigor

**Trio**  Cleo Leo Rio

**Trip**  battleship chip clip dip drip equip flip grip gyp hip lip nip
quip rip scrip ship slip snip strip tip whip zip

**Trooper**  cooper hooper looper snooper stupor super

**Trot**  (see **Pot**)

**Troubadour**  (see **Door**)

**Trouble**  bubble double rubble stubble

**Troublemaker**  (see **Acre**)

**Truce**  caboose goose loose moose noose papoose recluse
spruce vamoose

**Truck**  amuck buck chuck cluck deduct duck horror-struck
luck muck pluck potluck puck struck suck tuck

**Trucker**  bucker chucker clucker pucker sapsucker
seersucker sucker (see *her*)

**True**  (see **Do**)

**Truest**  bluest newest

**T**

**Truly**  coolie coolly duly newly ruly unduly unruly

**Trumpet**  bump it crumpet dump it lump it strumpet
thump it

**Trunk**  bunk chunk clunk cyberpunk drunk dunk flunk
funk hunk junk monk plunk punk shrunk skunk slunk
spunk stunk sunk

**Trust**  adjust August bust crust disgust distrust
encrust entrust gust just lust mistrust must robust
rust thrust unjust

**Truth** booth couth Duluth sleuth tooth uncouth youth

**Try** alibi amplify banzai barfly butterfly buy by bye certify
clarify crucify cry defy deify deny die dignify diversify
dragonfly drive-by dry dye eye firefly fly fry glorify gratify
guy high horrify I identify imply July justify lie lullaby
modify my mystify notify passerby pie pry qualify rely
rye satisfy sci-fi shy sigh signify simplify sky sly specify spry
spy terrify testify thigh tie underlie verify why

**Tub** Beelzebub bub club cub grub hub hubbub pub rub
rub-a-dub-dub scrub shrub snub stub sub

**Tube** boob cube rube

**Tug** bug drug dug jug hug lug mug plug pug rug shrug slug
smug snug thug

**Tuition** (see **Tradition**)

**Tulip** julep

**Tumor** bloomer boomer consumer humor rumor

**Tune** attune commune dune immune impugn
inopportune June (see *moon*)

**Tunnel** funnel

**Turf** nerf serf surf

**Turkey** Albuquerque murky perky quirky

**Turmoil** broil coil foil loyal oil recoil royal spoil toil

**Turn** adjourn burn churn concern discern earn fern
intern kern learn overturn return sojourn spurn stern
taciturn urn yearn

**Turtle** fertile girdle myrtle

**Tusk** dusk husk musk

**Twice** advice concise device dice entice ice lice mice nice
paradise precise price rice sacrifice spice splice suffice
thrice vice

**Twilight** highlight skylight (see *light*)

**T**

**Twin**  (see **Been**)

**Twinkle**  crinkle periwinkle sprinkle tinkle wrinkle

**Twirp**  blurp burp chirp usurp Wyatt Earp

**Twist**  (see **Mist**)

**Twisted**  assisted cysted enlisted existed fisted insisted listed
misted persisted resisted subsisted

**Twister**  assister blister magister mister
resister sister (see *her*)

**Type**  archetype gripe hype pipe prototype ripe stereotype
stripe swipe wipe

**Tyrant**  aspirant

**T**

# U

**Udder**  rudder shudder

**Ugly**  smugly snugly

**Ulcer**  (see *her*)

**Ultimate**  befit bit fit 'git grit kit knit hit it lit mitt nit-wit pit quit sit twit unfit wit zit

**Umbrella**  Béla fella' Stella

**Ump**  bump chump clump dump hump jump lump plump rump slump stump thump trump

**Under**  blunder plunder thunder wonder

**Underdog**  analog bog catalog clog cog dog fog demagogue dialogue epilogue flog frog grog hog jog log monologue synagogue travelogue

**Undercover**  cover discover hover lover recover rediscover shover (see *her*)

**Understood**  brotherhood could fatherhood firewood good Hollywood hood likelihood livelihood misunderstood motherhood neighborhood should sisterhood stood understood withstood womanhood wood would

**Unicorn**  adorn airborne born Cape Horn Capricorn corn forlorn horn lovelorn Matterhorn morn mourn popcorn scorn seaborne stillborn sworn warn worn

**Uniform**  chloroform conform deform form inform norm perform rainstorm reform snowstorm storm swarm transform warm

**Union**  communion disunion reunion

**Unite**  blight cite delight excite ignite incite indict invite knight light recite requite reunite right sight spite

**Universal**  rehearsal reversal

**Universe**  adverse converse curse disburse disperse diverse
hearse immerse intersperse inverse nurse purse rehearse
reverse terse transverse traverse verse worse

**Until**  bill chill daffodil distill drill fill frill fulfill gill grill
hill ill imbecile instill kill mill nil quill shrill sill skill
spill still swill thrill till trill whippoorwill will
windmill windowsill

**Up**  buttercup cup fed up hard-up pick-up pup sup

**Upon**  Amazon Babylon begone bonbon Bonn brawn
chiffon con Don dawn drawn fawn gone hexagon John
lawn lexicon octagon on Oregon pawn pentagon silicon
undergone withdrawn wanton yawn

**Uproot**  (see **Shoot**)

**Upset**  alphabet bayonet bet brunette cabinet cadet cigarette
larinet cornet corvette debt duet forget fret gazette get
jet Joliet Juliet let luncheonette marionette met net
omelet pet quartet regret roulette set silhouette
Somerset sunset sweat threat Tibet toilette vet 'vette
violet wet yet

**Urge**  converge dirge diverge emerge merge purge scourge
serge splurge submerge surge verge

**Urgent**  detergent divergent emergent resurgent

**Urn**  (see **Learn**)

**Us**  *one syllable:*
bus cuss Gus muss plus pus truss thus

*two syllable:*
discuss

*three syllable:*
amorous barbarous blasphemous boisterous cancerous
cankerous cavernous chivalrous courteous curious

**U**

devious dubious envious hideous industrious infamous
lecherous ludicrous marvelous murderous nauseous
nautilus nebulous numerous octopus ominous omnibus
perilous poisonous ponderous precarious prosperous
ravenous rebellious rigorous riotous scandalous
scrupulous sensuous  curious devious dubious envious
hideous industrious infamous lecherous ludicrous
marvelous murderous nauseous nautilus nebulous
numerous octopus ominous omnibus perilous poisonous
ponderous precarious prosperous ravenous rebellious
rigorous riotous scandalous scrupulous sensuous serious
slanderous stimulus strenuous studious tedious
tempestuous thunderous tortuous treacherous
treasonous various villainous

*four or more syllable:*
adventurous ambiguous androgynous anonymous
conspicuous contemptuous continuous dangerous
delirious erroneous extraneous famous frivolous furious
fuss generous gregarious glorious gratuitous harmonious
hazardous hilarious illustrious incredulous luxurious
miscellaneous monogamous monotonous mysterious
notorious oblivious populous posthumous preposterous
presumptuous promiscuous simultaneous spontaneous
tumultuous uproarious victorious

**Use**　abuse accuse confuse cues deduce diffuse disuse duce
excuse induce infuse introduce juice misuse obtuse
peruse produce profuse reduce refuse reproduce
seduce Syracuse

**User**　abuse accuser boozer bruiser cruiser lose 'er loser
muser oozer refuse 'er refuser snoozer

**Utter**　butter clutter cutter flutter gutter mutter putter
shutter sputter strutter stutter

**U**

213

# V

**Vacate** (see **Ate**)

**Vague** plague

**Vain** abstain again airplane arraign ascertain attain brain Cain
campaign cane chain champagne cocaine complain contain
crane detain disdain domain drain entertain explain
feign gain grain humane hurricane hydroplane insane
lane main Maine maintain mane migraine obtain ordain
pain pane pertain plain plane profane propane rain refrain
reign rein remain sane slain Spain sprain stain strain
sustain train vane vein wane windowpane

**Valid** ballad invalid salad

**Valley** alley dilly-dally rally Sally tally

**Vamp** amp camp champ clamp cramp damp lamp ramp stamp

**Vandal** candle dandle handle sandal scandal

**Vanilla** gorilla guerrilla Manila Priscilla villa

**Variety** anxiety impropriety notoriety piety propriety
sobriety society (see **Be**)

**Various** (see **Us**)

**Vary** carry hari-kari marry miscarry parry (see _cherry_)

**Vase** ace base bass brace case chase commonplace debase
disgrace displace embrace encase erase face grace lace
mace misplace pace place race replace space steeplechase
trace unlace

**Vast** aghast blast cast classed contrast fast flabbergast forecast
gassed last mast outlast overcast passed past

**Vat** (see **At**)

**Vault** assault cobalt exalt fault halt malt salt somersault

**Vegetarian**  Aquarian Aryan barbarian buryin' Cesarean
disciplinarian ferryin' humanitarian libertarian librarian
Marion marryin' Sagittarian Unitarian veterinarian

**Veil**  (see **Ale**)

**Vendor**  (see **Tender**)

**Vent**  (see **Bent**)

**Venture**  adventure denture indenture misadventure

**Verb**  blurb 'burb curb disturb herb perturb Serb
suburb superb

**Verbal**  gerbil herbal

**Verbose**  adios bellicose close comatose diagnose
dose engross grandiose gross morose nose
overdose varicose

**Verge**  converge dirge diverge emerge merge purge scourge
serge splurge submerge surge urge

**Vermin**  determine German merman sermon

**Verse**  adverse converse curse disburse disperse diverse
hearse immerse intersperse inverse nurse purse rehearse
reverse terse transverse traverse universe worse

**Vessel**  nestle trestle wrestle

**Veto**  bonito mosquito neat-o

**Viaduct**  abduct conduct construct deduct instruct obstruct
plucked viaduct

**Vice**  advice concise device dice entice ice lice mice nice
paradise precise price rice sacrifice spice splice suffice
thrice twice

**Vicious**  ambitious auspicious capricious delicious expeditious
factious fictitious judicious malicious nutritious propitious
seditious superstitious suspicious

**Victory**  (see **Be**)

**View**  adieu anew avenue barbecue bayou chew choo-choo
     cue curfew debut dew due ensue ewe few guru
     honeydew hue I.O.U. imbue ingénue interview Jew knew
     lieu new Nehru overdue pee-ewe pew preview pursue
     renew residue revenue review spew subdue sue undue
     yew you (see *do*)

**Vigor**  bigger chigger digger rigger rigor swigger tigger trigger

**Vile**  aisle awhile beguile bile compile crocodile defile file isle
     juvenile meanwhile mile Nile pile rile smile style tile while
     wile worthwhile

**Village**  pillage tillage

**Villain**  billin' chillin' Dylan fillin' illin' willin' (see *in*)

**Vindictive**  (see **Native**)

**Vine**  (see **Fine**)

**Violate**  (see **Ate**)

**Violence**  (see **Fence**)

**Viper**  bagpiper pied piper riper sniper striper swiper
     typer wiper

**Virgin**  burgeon emergin' mergin' sturgeon surgeon
     surgin' urgin'

**Virginity**  (see **Be**)

**Visible**  divisible indivisible invisible

**Vision**  collision decision derision division incision indecision
     precision provision revision supervision television

**Vital**  entitle recital title

**Vivid**  livid

**Vocal**  focal local yokel

**Vogue**  brogue rogue

**Voice**  choice invoice rejoice

**Void**  avoid alkaloid asteroid joyed Lloyd Sigmund Freud
     tabloid toyed

V

**Volcanic**　Hispanic manic mechanic monomaniac oceanic
organic panic satanic titanic (see *romantic*)

**Volley**　collie dolly finale folly golly jolly melancholy Molly Polly
tamale trolley

**Voodoo**　(see **Do**)

**Vote**　afloat antidote bloat boat coat connote denote dote
float footnote gloat goat misquote moat note oat
overcoat promote quote remote riverboat rote smote
throat tote underwrote wrote

**Vouch**　couch crouch grouch ouch pouch slouch

**Vow**　allow avow bough bow brow chow cow disavow endow
frau how kowtow now ow plough plow row slough
somehow sow thou wow

**Vowel**　bowel dowel towel trowel

**Vulture**　agriculture culture

# W

**Wag**  bag brag drag flag gag hag lag mag nag rag sag shag slag
snag stag swag tag

**Wage**  age cage gage page rampage sage stage

**Waif**  safe

**Wait**  (see **Ate**)

**Wake**  ache bake brake break cake fake flake forsake headache
heartache keepsake make mistake opaque quake rake
shake snake stake steak take

**Walk**  Bangkok beanstalk boondock cock cornstalk clock
crock deadlock defrock dock flintlock flock frock gawk
gridlock hawk hock J. S. Bach jock knock Little Rock
livestock lock mock Mohawk padlock peacock rock
shock sidewalk small talk smock sock squawk stalk stock
talk tomahawk unlock wok

**Wall**  all ball bawl brawl call crawl doll drawl fall gall haul
install mall maul Montreal nightfall overhaul parasol pitfall
protocol rainfall scrawl shawl small snowfall sprawl stall
tall thrall waterfall y'all

**Wallow**  Apollo follow hollow swallow

**Wand**  beyond blond bond correspond fond dawned pond
respond spawned vagabond yawned

**Wander**  condor conned 'er fonder launder ponder
squander yonder

**Want**  daunt flaunt gaunt haunt jaunt taunt

**Ward**  (see **Lord**)

**Warm**  chloroform conform deform form inform norm
perform rainstorm reform snowstorm storm swarm
transform uniform

W

**Wart** abort assort cavort comfort contort court davenport deport distort escort exhort export extort fort import passport port quart report resort retort short snort sort sport support thwart tort transport (see **Art**)

**Wary** adversary airy arbitrary beneficiary berry bury canary capillary cautionary cherry commentary culinary customary dairy dictionary dietary dignitary disciplinary discretionary evolutionary extraordinary fairy February ferry functionary hairy hereditary honorary imaginary incendiary intermediary January Jerry legendary legionary literary luminary Mary mercenary military momentary monetary mortuary nary necessary obituary ordinary Perry planetary prairie proprietary pulmonary reactionary revolutionary sanctuary sanitary scary secretary seminary sherry solitary stationary temporary Terry Tipperary very visionary vocabulary voluntary

**Was** abuzz buzz cause coz does fuzz

**Was** applause because cause clause claws gauze laws menopause Oz pause paws Santa Claus

**Wash** awash frosh galosh gosh hogwash josh Macintosh posh quash slosh squash swash

**Waste** baste aftertaste braced chaste distaste faced freckle-faced haste hatchet-faced lambaste paste taste two-faced waist

**Watch** blotch botch crotch debauch hopscotch notch Scotch wristwatch

**Water** blotter daughter hotter otter plotter slaughter spotter squatter trotter

**Wave** behave brave cave concave crave engrave forgave gave grave knave pave rave save shave slave waive

**Wax** ax backs fax jacks lax max relax packs Saks sax slacks tax

**Way**　array bay betray bluejay bouquet bray clay day decay
delay disarray dismay display eh? essay exposé fray gay
gray hay hey holiday hooray José Kay lay matinee may
moiré naysay negligée obey pay play portray protégé ray
résumé ricochet risqué rosé say slay sleigh soufflé stay
stray sway they toupee weigh x-ray

**We**　(see **Be**)

**Wealth**　commonwealth health stealth

**Weary**　bleary cheery deary dreary eerie Erie leery
query teary

**Weasel**　diesel easel measle

**Weather**　altogether feather Heather leather tether
together whether (see *her*)

**Weave**　achieve believe bereave conceive disbelieve eve
grieve heave leave perceive receive relieve reprieve
retrieve sleeve

**Web**　deb ebb

**Wed**　ahead bed bedspread bread bred coed dead dread fed
figurehead fled flowerbed fountainhead gingerbread head
inbred lead led misled misread overfed read red riverbed
said shed shred sled sped spread thoroughbred thread
underfed unthread

**Wedge**　allege dredge edge fledge hedge ledge privilege
sacrilege sledge

**Weed**　agreed breed centipede concede creed deed exceed
feed greed heed inbreed knead lead mislead need precede
proceed read recede reed secede seed speed stampede
succeed Swede tweed

**Weep**　barkeep cheep creep deep heap keep leap peep reap
seep sheep sleep steep sweep

**W**

**Weight**  (see **Ate**)

**Weighty**  eighty Haiti matey

**Weird**  appeared beard cleared disappeared feared jeered
neared persevered smeared speared

**Welch**  belch squelch

**Weld**  felled held meld upheld

**Well**  bell belle Carmel carrousel cell clientele dell dwell excel
farewell fell gel hell hotel infidel knell mademoiselle
personnel sell shell smell spell tell yell

**Welt**  belt Celt dealt felt heartfelt melt pelt

**Went**  (see **Bent**)

**Wept**  accept adept crept except intercept kept overslept
slept stepped swept

**Were**  amateur blur chauffeur concur confer connoisseur
defer demur deter fur her incur infer inter myrrh
occur per prefer purr recur sir slur spur stir transfer
voyageur whir

**Wet**  alphabet bayonet bet brunette cabinet cadet cigarette
clarinet cornet corvette debt duet epithet etiquette
forget fret gazette get jet Joliet Juliet let luncheonette
marionette net omelet pet quartet regret roulette set
silhouette Somerset sunset sweat threat Tibet toilette
upset vet 'vette violet yet

**Wharf**  dwarf

**What**  (see **But**, **Hot**)

**Wheat**  (see **Sweet**)

**Wheel**  appeal automobile Bastille Camille conceal deal eel
feel genteel he'll heal heel ideal kneel meal mobile peel
real reel repeal reveal seal she'll spiel squeal steal steel
veal we'll zeal

**Where** affair air anywhere aware bare bear billionaire blare
care chair compare dare debonair declare despair
disrepair elsewhere everywhere fair fare flair glare hair
hare heir impair legionnaire mare midair millionaire
nightmare pair pare pear Pierre prayer prepare rare
ready-to-wear repair scare snare solitaire somewhere
spare square stair stare swear tear their there
thoroughfare unaware underwear unfair ware wear

**Which** bewitch bitch ditch enrich glitch hitch pitch rich snitch
stitch switch twitch

**Whiff** cliff handkerchief if sniff stiff tiff

**While** aisle awhile beguile bile compile crocodile defile file
isle juvenile meanwhile mile Nile pile rile smile style tile
vile wile worthwhile

**Whim** brim dim grim gym hymn limb pseudonym skim slim
swim trim

**Whimper** scrimper shrimper skimper

**Whip** battleship chip clip dip drip equip flip grip gyp hip lip
nip quip rip scrip ship slip snip strip tip trip zip

**Whirl** curl earl girl hurl pearl swirl twirl

**Whisker** brisker frisker risker

**Whiskey** frisky risky

**Whisper** crisper (see *her*)

**Whistle** bristle dismissal gristle missal missile sisal thistle

**White** (see **Fight**)

**Whiz** biz fizz friz his is quiz showbiz 'tis

**Whole** bowl buttonhole cajole casserole coal control dole
droll enroll goal hole loophole Maypole mole Old King
Cole oriole parole patrol pole poll porthole role roll
scroll tadpole toll troll

**W**

**Whom**  bloom boom broom cloakroom doom entomb flume
    gloom groom room tomb womb zoom

**Whopper**  (see **Proper**)

**Whose**  blues booze bruise choose cruise lose news ooze
    shoes snooze

**Why**  alibi amplify banzai barfly butterfly buy by bye certify
    clarify crucify cry defy deify deny die dignify diversify
    dragonfly drive-by dry dye eye firefly fly fry glorify gratify
    guy high horrify I identify imply July justify lie lullaby
    modify my mystify notify passerby pie pry qualify rely
    rye satisfy sci-fi shy sigh signify simplify sky sly specify
    spry spy terrify testify thigh tie try underlie verify

**Wick**  arithmetic arsenic brick candlestick candlewick
    Catholic chick click flick heartsick hick kick lick limerick
    love-sick lunatic maverick music nick pick sick slick stick
    thick tic tick

**Wide**  beside bonafide bride collide confide countryside
    decide defied died dignified divide eyed fireside guide
    hide hillside homicide inside lied outside override pride
    provide reside ride side slide snide stride subdivide
    subside suicide tide tried yuletide

**Wider**  chider cider decider divider glider insider low-rider
    outsider provider rider slider spider

**Wield**  battlefield Chesterfield field shield yield

**Wife**  afterlife jackknife knife life strive wife

**Wig**  big dig fig gig jig pig renege rig swig thingamajig twig

**Wiggle**  giggle jiggle squiggle wriggle

**Wild**  child dialed mild piled smiled

**Will**  bill chill daffodil distill drill frill fulfill gill grill hill ill
    imbecile instill kill mill nil quill shrill sill skill spill still swill
    thrill till trill until whippoorwill will windmill windowsill

**Willing** billing chilling distilling drilling filling fulfilling instilling
killing milling shrilling spilling stilling swilling thrilling
tilling unwilling

**Willow** armadillo billow peccadillo pillow

**Wilt** built guilt hilt jilt kilt quilt spilt stilt tilt Vanderbilt

**Wimp** blimp gimp limp pimp shrimp skimp

**Win** again aspirin been begin Berlin bin chagrin chin discipline
feminine fin genuine gin grin harlequin heroine in inn kin
mandolin mannequin masculine moccasin origin pin
saccharine shin sin skin spin thick-and-thin thin tin twin
violin within

**Wind** behind bind blind find grind hind humankind kind
mastermind mind remind signed unkind unwind wined

**Wind** disciplined grinned rescind sinned (see *bend*)

**Wine** (see **Fine**)

**Wing** anything bring cling ding evening everything fling
king ring sing sling spring sting string swing thing wring
(add "ing" to "action" words, i.e., run(ning), etc.)

**Wink** blink brink chink clink drink fink ink kink link mink pink
rink shrink sink slink stink zinc

**Winner** B. F. Skinner beginner breadwinner dinner inner
sinner skinner spinner thinner

**Wino** albino rhino (see *know*)

**Winter** hinter printer splinter sprinter squinter
tinter (see *her*)

**Wipe** archetype gripe hype pipe prototype ripe stereotype
stripe swipe type

**Wiping** griping piping stereotyping striping swiping typing

**Wire** acquire admire amplifier aspire attire buyer choir
conspire crier cryer desire dire drier dryer entire
esquire expire fire flier friar higher hire inquire inspire

**W**

justifier liar magnifier multiplier mystifier perspire prior
prophesier require retire satisfier sire squire supplier
testifier tire transpire

**Wise** (see **Lies**)

**Wiser** advertiser adviser agonizer analyzer apologizer
equalizer eulogizer exerciser fertilizer geyser harmonizer
idolizer miser riser sizer surpriser

**Wish** devilish dish fish gibberish impoverish squish swish

**Wisp** crisp lisp

**Wit** befit bit fit 'git grit kit knit hit it lit nit-wit pit quit
sit twit unfit zit

**Witchcraft** craft draft draught graft overdraft

**Witches** bitches ditches enriches hitches itches niches
pitches riches stitches switches twitches

**Witty** city committee ditty gritty kitty pity pretty self-pity

**Wizard** gizzard lizard scissored

**Woe** (see **Blow**)

**Woes** arose chose close compose decompose depose
disclose dispose doze enclose expose foreclose froze
goes hose impose indispose interpose knows nose owes
pose predispose presuppose prose recompose rose
suppose those toes transpose

**Woke** artichoke baroque bloke broke choke cloak coke
croak evoke folk invoke joke oak poke provoke revoke
smoke soak spoke stroke toke yoke

**Womb** bloom boom broom cloakroom doom entomb flume
gloom groom room tomb whom zoom

**Wonder** blunder plunder under thunder

**Wool** bull cock-and-bull do-able full pull (see *beautiful*)

**Word** absurd bird blackbird bluebird curd heard herd
Kurd hummingbird ladybird mockingbird overheard
third yellowbird

**Work**  clerk handiwork irk jerk Kirk lurk murk overwork
      perk quirk shirk smirk Turk

**Worker**  book 'er hook 'er lurker shirker shook 'er smirker
      snooker took 'er (see *her*)

**World**  underworld

**Worm**  affirm confirm firm germ reaffirm sperm squirm term

**Worn**  adorn airborne born Cape Horn Capricorn corn
      forlorn horn lovelorn Matterhorn morn mourn popcorn
      scorn seaborne stillborn sworn unicorn warn

**Worry**  curry flurry fury hurry jury Missouri scurry
      slurry surrey

**Worse**  adverse converse curse disburse disperse diverse
      hearse immerse intersperse inverse nurse purse rehearse
      reverse terse transverse traverse universe verse

**Worst**  burst cursed first nursed outburst thirst versed

**Worth**  birth dearth earth girth mirth

**Would**  brotherhood could fatherhood firewood good
      Hollywood hood likelihood livelihood misunderstood
      motherhood neighborhood should sisterhood stood
      understood withstood womanhood wood

**Wound**  (see **Sound**)

**Woven**  Beethoven cloven interwoven

**Wow**  allow avow bough bow brow chow cow disavow
      endow frau how kowtow now ow plough plow row
      slough somehow sow thou vow

**Wrap**  cap chap clap flap gap handicap lap map mishap nap rap
      sap scrap slap snap strap tap trap zap

**W**

**Wrapper**  capper clapper dapper flapper handicapper
      rapper slapper snapper tapper whippersnapper
      wiretapper yapper

**Wrath**  aftermath bath homeopath math path
      psychopath sociopath

**Wreck**  check Czech deck fleck heck neck peck Quebec
     speck trek

**Wrecker**  checker chequer decker double-decker exchequer
     pecker woodpecker

**Wrench**  bench clench drench French monkey wrench quench
     stench trench wench

**Wrestle**  nestle trestle vessel

**Wretch**  catch etch fetch kvetch retch sketch stretch wretch

**Wring**  (see **Sing**)

**Wrinkle**  crinkle periwinkle sprinkle tinkle twinkle

**Wrist**  (see **Mist**)

**Write**  appetite bite blight bright byte contrite copyright
     daylight delight despite dynamite excite Fahrenheit
     fight flight fright headlight height ignite invite kite knight
     light midnight might moonlight night outright parasite
     plight polite quite recite reunite right satellite sight site
     sleight slight spite starlight sunlight tight trite twilight
     unite white

**Written**  bitten Britain Briton kitten mitten smitten (see *in*)

**Wrong**  along belong bong ding-dong gong Hong Kong long
     Ping-Pong prong song strong throng

**Wrote**  afloat antidote bloat boat coat connote denote dote
     float footnote gloat goat misquote moat note oat
     overcoat promote quote remote riverboat rote smote
     throat tote underwrote vote

**Wrought**  (see **Thought**)

# X

**X-rated**  (see **Hated**)

**X-ray**  array away bay betray bluejay bouquet bray clay day
decay delay disarray dismay display eh? essay exposé
fray gay gray hay hey holiday hooray José Kay lay matinee
may moiré naysay negligée obey pay play portray protégé
ray résumé ricochet risqué rosé say slay sleigh soufflé say
stay stray sway they toupee way weigh

**Xerox**  box chickenpox equinox fox mailbox orthodox ox
paradox rocks socks stocks

**Xylophone**  (see **Alone**)

# Y

**Yacht**  apricot blot Camelot clot cot cybot dot forget-me-not forgot fought gavotte got hot hot-shot jot knot lot not plot pot robot rot shot slingshot somewhat spot squat swat tot trot watt what

**Yank**  bank blank clank crank dank drank flank frank hank outrank plank prank rank sank shrank spank stank tank thank

**Yankee**  cranky hanky lanky

**Yard**  avant-garde card chard discard disregard guard hard lard regard retard tarred

**Yarn**  barn darn

**Yawn**  Amazon Babylon begone bonbon Bonn brawn chiffon con Don dawn drawn fawn gone hexagon John lawn lexicon octagon on Oregon pawn pentagon silicon undergone upon withdrawn wanton

**Year**  adhere appear atmosphere auctioneer beer bombardier career cashier cavalier chandelier cheer clear dear deer disappear ear engineer fear financier frontier gear hear hemisphere here insincere interfere jeer lavaliere leer mere mountaineer near overhear overseer peer persevere pioneer queer racketeer reappear rear revere seer severe shear sheer sincere smear sneer spear sphere stratosphere tear veneer volunteer

**Yearn**  adjourn burn churn concern discern earn fern intern kern learn overturn return sojourn spurn stern taciturn turn urn

**Yell**  bell belle Carmel carrousel cell clientele dell dwell excel farewell fell gel hell hotel infidel knell mademoiselle personnel sell shell smell spell tell well

**Yellow**  bellow cello fellow hello mellow Othello

**Yelp**  help kelp

**Yes** access address baroness bashfulness bitterness bless caress chess cleverness cloudiness compress confess craziness deadliness depress digress distress dizziness dress duress eagerness easiness eeriness emptiness excess express finesse foolishness ghostliness guess happiness haziness homelessness idleness impress joyfulness joylessness laziness less limitless Loch Ness lustfulness mess nervousness obsess openness oppress outrageousness penniless playfulness possess press profess progress queasiness recess regress repossess repress rockiness seediness shallowness silkiness sleaziness sleepiness sneakiness SOS spaciousness spitefulness stress success suppress thoughtfulness transgress uselessness viciousness willingness wishfulness worldliness youthfulness

**Yet** alphabet bayonet bet brunette cabinet cadet cigarette clarinet cornet corvette debt duet epithet etiquette forget fret gazette get jet Joliet Juliet let luncheonette marionette net omelet pet quartet regret roulette set silhouette Somerset sunset sweat threat Tibet toilette upset vet 'vette violet wet

**Yield** battlefield Chesterfield field shield wield

**Yodel** modal nodal

**Yoga** Saratoga toga

**Yogurt** (see **Shirt**)

**Yoke** (see **Joke**)

**Yonder** condor conned 'er fonder launder ponder squander wander

**You** adieu anew avenue barbecue bayou chew choo-choo cue curfew debut dew due ensue ewe few guru honeydew hue I.O.U. imbue ingénue interview Jew knew lieu new Nehru overdue pee-ewe pew preview pursue renew residue revenue review spew subdue sue undue view yew (see *do*)

**Young**  among clung dung flung high-strung hung lung rung
slung sprung strung stung sung swung tongue unstrung
unsung wrung

**Your**  (see **Door**)

**Your**  allure armature assure brochure caricature cocksure
cure demure endure ensure expenditure immature
impure insecure insure liqueur literature lure manicure
manure mature miniature obscure overture pedicure
premature pure reassure secure signature sure
tablature temperature

**Yourself**  elf herself himself itself myself self shelf

**Youth**  booth couth Duluth sleuth tooth truth uncouth

**Yum**  album aquarium auditorium become bum burdensome
Christendom come cranium crematorium crumb
curriculum drum dump emporium fee-fi-fo-fum glum gum
gymnasium hum kettledrum kingdom martyrdom
maximum meddlesome medium millennium minimum
mum museum numb opium overcome pendulum
petroleum platinum plum premium quarrelsome radium
random rum sanitarium scum slum some strum succumb
sum swum tedium thumb Tom Thumb Tweedledum
uranium worrisome yum

**Yuppie**  guppy puppy

# Z

**Zany**  brainy grainy rainy

**Zap**  cap chap clap flap gap handicap lap map mishap nap rap
sap scrap slap snap strap tap trap wrap

**Zeal**  (see **Wheel**)

**Zealous**  jealous sell us tell us (see *us*)

**Z**

**Zebra**  duh Ophra (see *raw*)

**Zen**  amen citizen den fen hen hydrogen Ken oxygen pen
regimen specimen ten then yen

**Zinc**  blink brink chink clink drink fink ink kink link mink pink
rink shrink sink slink stink think wink

**Zip**  battleship chip clip dip drip equip flip grip gyp hip lip nip
quip rip scrip ship slip snip strip tip trip whip

**Zit**  befit bit fit 'git grit kit knit hit it lit mitt nit-wit pit quit sit
twit unfit ultimate wit zit

**Zodiac**  (see **Track**)

**Zone**  alone atone backbone baritone blown bone chaperone
clone condone cone cornerstone cyclone Dictaphone
flown full-blown full-grown gramophone grindstone
groan grown headstone known loan lone microphone
milestone moan monotone mown overgrown overthrown
own phone postpone prone saxophone sewn shown
stone telephone thrown tone trombone unknown
xylophone zone

**Zoo**  accrue ado bamboo blew blue boo boohoo brew caribou
cashew clue construe coo coup crew cuckoo do drew
flew flue glue gnu goo grew Hindu hitherto hullabaloo
igloo impromptu into issue Kalamazoo kangaroo kazoo
kickapoo misconstrue moo outdo overdo overthrew
peekaboo Peru poo rendezvous screw shampoo shoe
shoo shrew Sioux slew slue stew taboo tattoo threw
through tissue to too true two undo voodoo wahoo
well-to-do who withdrew woo yahoo zoo Zulu (see *you*)

**Zoom**  bloom boom broom cloakroom doom entomb flume
gloom groom room tomb whom womb

**Z**